Ramblings of a Pantsless Canadian Old Guy

Blogs, Columns and Blah, Blah, Blah...

Gerald LaHay

This is a work of non-fiction. I have tried to keep most folks I refer to in these writings anonymous.

This book is a protected work, completely owned by Oldguysmusing. Reproduction is strictly prohibited. Besides, the book isn't that great so don't waste your time.

© Oldguysmusing

Welcome to Ramblings!

Inspired by someone that has been following my online blog, it was suggested that I publish a book. It seems, I have some interesting things to say.

In this book, you'll find some previously published writings, punched up a little as I always seem to either forget to include a thought while writing, or I've re-read what I've written and thought, "what the hell was I saying?"

The success of my writings is all thanks to you, the reader. My family, friends, and complete strangers have started to follow along with these weird, off the cuff blatherings. My life and what I have to say are not overly unique, but they are from my heart, my experiences in life and sometimes, I have nothing better to do!

I cannot thank those you enough. I dedicate this book to you! I hope you enjoy, learn and maybe laugh along the way!

Gerry

My First Column!

Welcome to The View from Oxford & Maitland!

I've always wanted to write a blog. Life was always too busy to sit and write or I'd find some excuse not to do it. Now, as a semi-retired, no pants wearing one legged old guy, I have the time.

This blog, to be published randomly, will present thoughts, concerns and general musings. This blog will chronicle some of what I have observed about life away from the cozy suburbs. Hope you enjoy.

I lived in Byron for close to 20 years. Living in the 'burbs, working 90 hour work weeks, coaching my amazing kids (they're no longer little ones!), volunteer work and life in general kept me too busy. I thought I knew a lot about London Ontario, but discovered very quickly I was wrong. My hectic, car driving lifestyle came with some unfriendly thoughts. Cyclists were a pain in the rear, pedestrians simply got in my way as I bombed around town in my Impala, the LTC was a poorly run, overcrowded and time consuming mode of transportation. I hadn't taken a bus in nearly 30 years! Since I never really thought about it, London, in my mind, didn't have a homeless problem, mental health issues were not a big deal and drug addiction wasn't really a problem. Had no sympathy for alcoholics and drug addicts. Alcoholics were the shady dudes in trench coats drinking booze out of a paper bag. They all needed to be stronger...stop being so damn weak.

Living in the heart of Byron, our property was quite large and private. Didn't really pay attention to the neighbours, I just wanted to sit under my flowering crab tree once in a while and read a book and more importantly, be left alone. I watched the local news each night. My street got plowed regularly in the winter and my garbage picked up right on schedule. But still, when I was angry with something, I blamed The City as everything was their fault.

I owned an old Canadian Tire Supercycle that, as a rule, sat in the garage, buried somewhere collecting dust. Walk to the store that was three blocks away? Ha! Not a chance. Besides, my twice a year walk through Springbank Park and the occasional walk with my dog Maisy was enough walking and I went to the gym each morning at five in the morning (something I started in 2004 when I weighed well over 400 pounds.), so I was getting enough exercise. I drove everywhere and complained, like everyone else when gas prices went up.

I knew there was some history in London, but as a history student, I focused on Canada and the World. I thought our downtown was a disaster with nothing to offer. Everything I needed was in a mall in Masonville or White Oaks. I always bought my coffee at Tim Hortons and dined at chain restaurants (nothing wrong with these companies!). I was all about big business and consistency. Politically, I only focused on what would affect me….not the big picture. I voted during each and every election, voting along party lines, not really paying attention to platforms.

I was diagnosed with type 2 diabetes years ago, but didn't pay attention to it because nothing was going to happen to me. I was living in the suburbs safe and sound and I was invincible. I was a successful business person, a good dad, a great volunteer who had raised tens of thousands of dollars for charity and overall, a good guy…in my mind. A Leafs fan and a

Star Wars junkie to boot with a son who loved Star Wars as much as his dad.

I was living the dream. House, a career where I was climbing the ladder, terrific family with two brilliant kids who are amazing athletes and are also incredible citizens, lots of friends, two cars in the driveway, trips to Florida every year and all the cool gadgets I could wish for. I owned the latest 55" Panasonic television with surround sound while enjoying a cable package that had every channel known to man...even the Swiss Chalet Channel. Along with our dog Maisy, I had two cats. I had a great pension so my future was secure.

I cut the grass on weekends, golfed when I could, hung the Christmas lights in the late fall (after bitching about the 40 bags of leaves I had just picked up), while enjoying a backyard campfire and had the life I had wished for. A self made man who had everything.

That would all change July 9th, 2016. This is where the story begins where now....I have almost nothing.....or so I thought.

And Now the Story Begins....

In last week's story, I mentioned that life would change for me in a dramatic way on July 9th, 2016 and it did. But in order to tell the story properly, I have to back up a bit. For reasons I won't get into, I separated from my wife and moved out September 2015. In the 28 years I was married, I drank alcohol on occasion, but rarely got drunk. A bottle of Bacardi would last months. Being a family guy, coaching my kids, work and volunteering were my focus. When I moved out, I started to live life in a different fashion. Bar hopping, dancing and dining out were new to me and to say I overindulged is an understatement.

A friend of mine calls me 110% Gerry. When I do something, I go full speed. My drinking started off with a few drinks, then a few more were needed. Breakfast Caesars were amazing. A trip to Cuba in January 2016 is a bit of a margarita blur. I was now drinking because I needed to....not because I wanted to have fun. As the months went on, my drinking was out of control. From vodka, rum, Jager, Tequila and Fireball, I was drinking it all. In mid June 2016, after cutting the grass, I changed into my trusty flip flops and cut my toe. Being a diabetic with neuropathy, I didn't feel it. Having noticed the blood, I slapped on a band aid and off I went. Guess I hadn't learned my lesson from previous infections. I kept it clean, kept on drinking to dull the pain and became a functioning alcoholic. I went to work to pay the rent and buy more booze. Work was important to me and I was proud of the work we were doing so I kept at it. The infection got worse, but I basically thought, as many of us do, it would get better on its own.

When I moved out, I weighed about 250. The drinking and infection took away any appetite but I didn't care. (My weight when I was admitted to hospital was down to 165). The infection was now way out of hand and my best friend kept encouraging me to go to the hospital. "It'll be fine" I would say while having another drink. On July 5th, I fainted in the shower. My best friend begged me to go to the hospital and I said I would once I sobered up. The next day I even packed a bag to go to the hospital, promising I would go. I started drinking again, this time because I knew what was coming. After repeatedly ignoring texts from my friend, there was a knock at my front door. Somewhat drunk, I opened the door to see my soon to be ex-wife and my daughter standing there. (I hadn't spoken to my ex for several months). I opened the door and nearly collapsed in her arms as I was so weak. The two of them grabbed me and my packed bag and dragged me to the hospital.

(Quick pause here: my ex-wife, my daughter and most importantly, my best friend saved my life although it took awhile to admit this.)

Arriving at LHSC, I was quickly hustled through triage and waited on a bed to be seen. I had a thought they would remove my toes. First doctor did an exam and ran some tests. Next thing I know, an Ortho resident showed up. He took one look, viewed test results and looked me in the eye and said "Mr. LaHay, we're going to have to amputate." I replied, "the toes rights?". He paused and simply and said "No, the whole foot". He showed me that they would be removing my leg mid shin. Stunned, I asked of there was no other option and he simply said no.

After being admitted, several residents and doctors came to see me. It had set in that I would lose the leg and while I didn't fully appreciate the gravity of the situation. The ortho surgeon advised me that I would be put on the surgery on call board, meaning I could be called at any time, therefore nothing to eat or drink. Thus, three days of hell began. I was on the on call list for three days, not being able to eat or drink anything. At the last minute each day, around 11:00 p.m., nurses would tell me that there wouldn't be a surgery. I basically had an hour to grab something to eat and drink as I'd be back on the nothing by mouth at midnight. I hustled down to cafeteria which was open all night to grab a quick bite.

Each day was the same. Worried about the surgery, waiting to be called at anytime, starving...and more waiting. Finally, on Saturday July 9th, I was advised I'd be heading to surgery at 8:00 p.m. I called my ex-wife to tell her as I knew my kids would be concerned about their dad. She reminded me that today, July the 9th, would have been our 28th wedding anniversary. Jokingly, she asked what made me more nervous, the surgery coming up or our wedding day? I immediately said our wedding day!

Having not really paid attention to time, nurses and porters showed up suddenly to take me to the operating room. Panic set in, but on the outside I remained calm. Hopping on to the stretcher, I resisted the urge to cry. This was really happening! Parked outside the operating room, I was left alone for a few minutes. My heart was racing and for a moment, I never felt so alone. A team of doctors showed up, we chatted for a second and then one of the surgeons pulled out a Sharpie. Confirming which leg was to be amputated, he signed the leg, said that the surgery would last less than an hour and then I was whisked into the operating room. The nurses and doctors all told me everything would be fine and that they'd take good care of me. Thankfully, I was sedated quickly and I was off to sleep.

This may be a tad graphic.

Waking up suddenly, I was in a pain that I've never felt. It was like I woke up mid surgery and they were cutting my leg off with a chainsaw. I could feel the metal chain cutting me. I was screaming and convulsing. I was swearing, screaming "mother******" over and over. One of the nurses yelled at me that language like that would not be tolerated. Another nurse grabbed me by the face and calmly said look at me and then asked the weirdest question: " Would you like a popsicle?" I was still very much in pain but said sure. Sucking on a peach popsicle seemed to make the pain go away. I then summoned up the courage to check my leg. Yep….it was gone. Surprisingly, I kept calm. The pain was gone and I was starting to feel good. The surgeon checked on me and after a while, I was taken back to my room.

Back in my room, I was feeling quite good. I changed out of the hospital gown into my usual t-shirt and shorts and then I need to go to the bathroom. The nurse brought me a urinal and I said I needed a wheelchair as I was going to use the bathroom, telling her for the sake of dignity, please let me. After arguing back and forth (I am a stubborn bastard/patient). I got my way, shifted into a wheelchair and off I went. Coming back out, the doctors were there along with the nurses to check on me. I was actually feeling good and told them I was starving and advised them I was going down to the Tim Hortons to grab something. The doctor asked if I was sure I was up to it and I replied that I was fine. He smiled and simply said "be careful." Off I went….

For the next three days of recovery, I was visited by doctors, nurses, a social worker, a physiotherapist student, friends and my son. When the staff changed the dressing, I couldn't look.

Therapy included about 5 minutes practising stairs, getting out of bed etc. I was feeling amazing, sober and a healthy appetite. Other than a patient with mental health issues attacking me (fought him off with crutches...looking back, I probably looked silly swinging the crutches, but it worked...).

As I mentioned earlier, I'm stubborn. And arrogant. And probably a little too self assured. I bombed around the hospital, keeping a positive mood. There is a long ram from the third floor of LHSC down to the parking lot. I'd start at the top, let go of the wheels and fly down the ramp. Problem was, it was a long climb back up the hill! Found out quickly how weak my upper body was at that time. After three days of laying around in the hospital, I wanted to go home. After a lengthy discussion with the doctors, they relented and agreed I could go home. I thought to myself, life in a wheelchair would be easy. After getting a ride home, and settling in, I was quite sure I could handle this. I would quickly learn, I was dead wrong.

The Steel Wheels Tour

No, I'm not talking about the terrific Stones album and tour of 1988 (Yep...saw them in Toronto. Second best concert I've ever seen!). Steel Wheels refers to life in a wheelchair, a life that lasted only 8 months....8 very long months. Before I continue, someone asked me why I'm writing these columns, stories, posts, blogs or whatever you want to call them. There is a point to this! I'm not going to disclosure my mission quite yet, but will soon!

Do you remember when you were a kid and you thought a wheelchair would be fun? Yeah...not so much I found out quickly. Oh, there were some fun moments, but for the most part, not an enjoyable experience.

Confident in my abilities, I went home three days after the surgery to remove my leg. As soon as I got home, I twinge of regret settled in. The house I was living in was a bungalow but both the front and rear entrances had several steps to climb. Here is where I learned to bum walk. Inside, I quickly discovered that my wheelchair was too wide, some doors I barely squeezed through. VON had been arranged so an OT quickly ordered a new, smaller chair and a shower bench. I would now shower sitting down. No one, including the professionals thought of grab bars for the bathroom, something I came to regret quite quickly. A nurse would drop by daily and randomly to change my dressing. A physiotherapist came weekly to ensure I was wrapping my stump properly in preparation for an eventual prosthetic leg. I would also complete a series of exercises to ensure my body was ready for a new leg.

When I got home, I had been sober for a few days. The goal was to get back to work at the golf course as quick as I could so I could start earning a paycheque again. I needed to prove I was as good as I was before the illness that cost me a leg. It was also summer and I don't like being kept inside. With the assistance of my greatest friend, I would venture back out into the world. Wow...did I learn a few things very quickly! First and foremost, London sidewalks aren't very wheelchair friendly, many of them in either poor repair or sloped on an angle. Add the fact that I was much weaker in my upper body than I realized. After all, I had lost a ton of weight and other than slugging beer kegs and cases at work, I really didn't use my arms much. I found trying to wheel one block exhausting. My friend ended up pushing me...something that needed to be done yet I hated it. When I would go out on my own, I was getting used to the chair, but did not get used to being hit by cars. Twice, drivers would back out, not see me, and bump into me.

Within the first couple of weeks, I fell a few times, a couple of times quite seriously. Once, I'm quite sure, I suffered a concussion when I fell in the bathroom. As a man, (yep...kind of dumb), I felt the need to stand to do my bathroom "business". I quickly discovered that this was simple unsafe and quite frankly, stupid. I cooked, cleaned, even bum walked downstairs to do laundry. I was getting used to this life. I got a second wheelchair for the Consistatory Club that I used outdoors. I would bum walk down the back stairs, hop into the second chair and off I'd go. I was getting around the neighbourhood quite well, including several trips to the LCBO near Grand Ave. Yes, I started to drink again, but it was "under control".

I learned to ride the LTC after not having ridden a bus in 30 years. I had to get to work and the LTC was really the only choice. I applied for Paratransit, but needed a doctor's certificate to prove I had lost a leg, even after going to the LTC office to apply and showing them my missing leg. I'm not going to spend time talking about Paratransit other than to say that I eventually did get approved, but quickly stopped using this service. To get Thames Valley Golf Course, I would take the number 4 bus downtown and then transfer to the #8. You know, when you drive all your life, you don't notice a lot of things, for example, the road to the club house is all DOWNHILL! I got off the bus, looked down the hill and went for it. Weeeeee.......! Wheelchairs don't have great breaks, none really, so my leg foot worked as a break. It wasn't too bad really. Kind of fun! Oh wait, its uphill to the bus stop to get home. No problem as the guys in the pro shop would strap my chair to the back of a golf cart and drive me up.

Even though the clubhouse has virtually no accessibility for wheelchairs, having been built in 1966, I managed. My wheelchair didn't fit through the doorway into the bar, so I'd simply stand up, hop into the bar and was quite capable of bartending. People were quite impressed that I could pour a pitcher...on one leg. I'd cook, tend bar, cater, manage, BBQ...no problem! There are several ladies golf leagues at Thames and they all treated me like gold. Two of the leagues raised money to help me cover expenses and one raised money for me to visit my best friend in North Bay. I was stunned at this wonderful support. Many friends helped me out with rides and a move to a disgusting dump of an apartment on Kipps Lane (didn't know it was so gross until I moved in...that's a whole different story).

I discovered that the LTC was eliminating the # 8 route. How in the hell was I going to get to work? I freaked and it was at this time that I realized life was catching up to me mentally. This is when I was diagnosed with anxiety and depression. Pouring over maps, I panicked but then I discovered that the #5 bus would get me close to the golf course to some degree. On the first day of taking the #5, I wheeled down Wonderland, made my way into the park, wheeled a couple of kilometres, over the bridge to the golf course. As I was wheeling through the park, I looked up and saw a very steep path leading up to the Civic Gardens that was close to the foot bridge over the Thames. This path would cut down quite bit of wheeling distance, so the next day I tried it. Wow...going downhill was like riding a coaster at Cedar Point...holy crap scary, yet fun at the same time. Going uphill to get home was a challenge. I learned to turn my chair around and go up backwards, using my left leg to push. The only thing was to not let go or I'd be back at the bottom quite quickly. Side note: love that there was a stop sign at the bottom of the hill. Not once was I going to stop...mainly because I couldn't! I swear I must have looked like a scene out of a comedy movie.

Life continued on and I managed to live life on my own in a wheelchair. Downtown leaves something to be desired though. Paving stone sidewalks in very poor repair, narrow sidewalks, some people not giving a damn about the guy in the wheelchair...that kind of stuff. Most stores are not wheelchair friendly, lacking ramps etc to get in. One store, the D&R Convenience Store (everyone knows this store!) is where I'd get bus tickets. Loved the staff here. I'd make my way over their step at the front door, open the door and make my way into the store. One day, I noticed they fixed the step and made a little cement ramp. I mentioned how great it was to the owners and they thanked me and said they did it for me!

I stayed sober in September and October of 2016. I went to work daily, took the buses home, and even started writing a book. The book, now published, is a crime fiction that takes place right in here in London Ontario! I was keeping busy and doing well. I faced quite a bit of discrimination as well. On two feet, I stand 6'2" and weigh 220. In a wheelchair, I looked small I guess. From being called a cripple to being harassed, I was a little alarmed. One time on the bus, as I was boarding, a woman could be heard "oh great, now we have to wait for the cripple guy to get strapped in". The bus driver was not amused and said so. Another time, a guy downtown asked me for money in exchange for, um, sexual favours. When I declined, he threatened to beat me up...until I stood up on one leg and told him, using colourful language, what would happen if he tried. But life continued.....

On November the 1st, as the golf season was winding down, I went off to work as usual. Early morning bus downtown, a stop at Starbucks for a coffee while I waited for a transfer, hop on the #8, ride down the hill at the Gardens and I was at work. They say that many of us, mostly men, don't listen to their bodies. Half an hour into my shift, I felt this stabbing pain in my chest. I became weak, and slumped over in my chair. I quickly came to and the pain in my chest grew more intense. An ambulance was called. I passed out in the ambulance, but the paramedics brought me back and informed me I was having a heart attack. I was rushed to University Hospital and quickly taken to the Angioplasty Lab when a team was waiting for my arrival. A blocked artery was quickly repaired with a stent. Doctors told me I had what was called a "widowmaker" and was minutes from death. Needless to say I didn't see that coming. After a couple of days, I was sent home, armed with a ton of new pills to take.

Recuperating at home, with the golf course closed, income was an issue. I had no idea where to turn. Speaking with my social worker, she pointed me in the direction. I would drink heavily when I could, sometimes passing out for what I thought was an hour, but turned out to be three days according to the police! I guess my benders were far worse than I thought as family and friends would call the police requesting a welfare check. At times, I was drinking 60oz of vodka a day. I'd sober up, detox on my own, and press forward for a few weeks.

In early February 2017, I had to go to the store. I got stuck in the snow in my wheelchair. People would ignore me and after several minutes, I planted my foot in the snow, stood up on one leg, lifted my wheelchair out of the snow and went home. I called Parkwood to see if I could be admitted into the amputee program to begin rehab with a prosthetic leg. Despite the initial $12,000 cost, I was determined to walk again. Five days later, I began the five week program (I did it in three weeks!). Amazing people and program. I went home three weeks later with a new leg...and was walking again!!!

For the next few weeks, I walked more and more, preparing to return to work. I admitted to myself I was an alcoholic and started attending AA meetings. I returned to work in March 2017 and things were sort of going well. Happy to be back on two feet, yet I was still very depressed and couldn't get happy. I started to drink again only this time, much heavier. 40oz turned to 60oz which turned to 80oz plus...a day! I'd start the day with coffee and Baileys in one hand and vodka in the other. One day, I was so hung over and sick, I made my way to the LCBO, grabbed a few bottles and a few Ceasars, sat at the bus stop, downing the booze like crazy, just so I could stop the shakes and make my way home to drink. I started missing work, ignoring everyone, locking myself in my apartment, only coming out to meet the delivery guy who would bring me my next load of alcohol. I don't remember many days, waking up to see empties everywhere. One time, my clothes were covered in blood. I vaguely remember falling and smashing my face on the floor....

Everyday, I was drunk and sinking deeper and deeper into depression until April 17th, 2017. This would be the worst day of my life.

I'm A Dead Man.... (Part One)

Previously, I said April 17th, 2017 was the worst day of my life, but it started shortly before that. Drinking was my way of life now. Every chance I could drink, I did. I was now drinking 60oz to 100oz of vodka, plus a 40 of Baileys a day. All I wanted was to get drunk, pass out and sleep away all of my worries.

My best friend knew something was obviously wrong. One night, she showed up at my place and found me wasted. She took my vodka and ran out the door with it, jumping into her car. Now, to get to the top of the garage, you had to climb a set of stairs. Even though I had a prosthetic leg, I was in my wheelchair. How I got up the stairs, I don't know. I was livid she had taken my booze. After she left, I had to get down the stairs. This part, I remember! I figured if I took a long run at it, I'd jump the stairs and land on my wheels. That didn't obviously work...I made it to the bottom but landed hard and painful. (Later determined I had a cracked rib and a very sore tail bone....don't ever attempt an Evil Knievel down a set of stairs kids!)

I started missing shifts at work. I was buying booze everyday. Where did the money come from to pay for so much alcohol? Certain life's luxuries didn't get paid, such as rent. In my mind, through a drunken haze, life was certainly a disaster. Not dealing with the mental issues that arose from an amputated leg, a heart attack, a divorce and guilt I felt for shutting myself in and hurting those around me led to a crash and an inevitable eviction. What was the point of going on? In the past, when I didn't drink, I was a sound thinker and very responsible. Not anymore.

I planned on killing myself April 17th. I worked with my aforementioned best friend and on Easter Sunday, April 16th, I completely screwed her and another friend, and walked off the job (yes...I was drunk). I told my best friend to leave me alone, in more colourful language. I went home, drank as much alcohol as possible and passed out. Waking up April 17th,, I finished off the alcohol, sat in my wheelchair by the patio doors and took a massive overdose of insulin and pills. Now I just had to wait to die.

As the day progressed, I felt my body start to go numb and I was losing all energy. I could barely move in my wheelchair. Hours later, through a very confused haze, I saw my best friend outside. As she tells me later, she was concerned about me and came to check on me. I let her in and then very slowly crawled into bed. At this point, she didn't know about the overdose. My blood sugar dropped to zero and I lost the ability to really move. I told my friend I had taken the overdose but I would be okay. A little later on, I woke up to my friend yelling at me. She thought I was having a heart attack and called 911. I thought I was coherent but I guess I wasn't at this point.

Paramedics showed up and I felt I was okay. My friend told them I had taken an insulin overdose. They asked how much and I replied 3 vials, equalling about 600 units. In truth I had taken 7 vials, about 1400 units, but I didn't admit that I as didn't want to go to the hospital. EMS indicated either I go with them to the hospital or go with the police, it was my choice. I elected to get on the stretcher and was rushed to the hospital. According to the paramedic who was taking care of me, I went unconscious for a brief moment. Once inside the hospital, I was brought to a pod. The next thing I remember, there was a team of doctors and nurses working on me...I seems I died for a moment. Over the next 48 hours, the medical staff in emerg checked my blood sugar every 30 minutes, giving me massive doses of glucose in order to bring my blood sugars back.

During this time, I was also being watched by security obviously for my own safety. During this 48 hour period, I was also suffering a major detox. Sweating, hallucinations and nausea were very intense. At one point, I walked down to the washroom and in a dizzy haze, I fell down. The door flew open as a team of security officers and nurses assisted me back to bed.

So, feeling incredibly sick already, I discovered the gentleman in the bed was suffering severe pain for an inability to go to the bathroom. Imagine how sick I was as they gave this poor guy an enema....and then just as I was uncontrollably sick, my poor son walks in. My boy has an iron stomach and was very understanding, but what a way to see your dad. Once I was somewhat stabilized, I was moved to a private room in critical care where, for the next couple of days, the staff nursed me back to health. It was on this ward that I was informed that I would be held under Form 3 under the Mental Health Act. Normally, I would have fought this, but it was at this moment I realized I needed help, so I resigned myself to staying for the next few days.

In CCU, I wasn't allowed to leave to go get a coffee or take a walk in the sunshine. I had my laptop, phone etc, so I just decided to ride this out. My best friend,(I'm tired of calling her my best friend. The name of my guardian angel is Nadine), family and another good friend came to visit. My butt was getting kicked with every visit....deservedly so. It was during one visit with Nadine who informed me that I was being evicted from my apartment. I figured it couldn't get any worse...this was the bottom. Nadine grabbed as much of my personal items as she could. My worldly possessions were now in two bags. I lost everything.

A couple of days later, now recovered and sober, I was moved to the 7th floor at LHSC, the adult mental health ward. My heart sank. Everything I knew of a mental health ward came from watching **One Flew Over the Cuckoo's Nest** too many times. Entering the secure ward, I noticed the glassed in nursing station and immediately got scared. I panicked once I was brought to my room. A private room with paint peeling on the walls. There was an alarm that sounded each time the bathroom door opened. I broke down in tears but was reassured by Nadine that this was a good thing and that I'd be okay. An orderly took away my two bags for inspection. When he returned, he had taken away all my electronic's cords, my shaving kit, and the picture frames from the two photos I had of Nadine and my kids. Surprisingly, I was allowed to keep my headphones. Nadine left for the evening and I was left alone. A nurse came in and sat to talk about what the routine on this floor would be like. They preferred meals to be eaten in a common dining room (I refused), medications would be given out at the desk etc. She took me for a tour of the ward. There are two wards actually, the 100 and the 200 wards. The 100 ward for was for those who needed less attention and were calmer. As we walked around, I noticed the various patients, older, younger, male, female and was surprised how many of us there were on this ward. The ward is locked, so I didn't have the ability to leave the floor. I retreated to my room and sat in a chair all night wondering how in the hell I got here.

The next morning, a psychiatrist and her resident visited to discuss my case. Obviously, I was suffering severe depression and anxiety. I was informed that in order to heal, I had to put some work into this program. Each day, there were various sessions that we were encouraged to attend. I was asked if I wanted to increase the very low dose anti-anxiety medication I was on and agreed on a slight increase. There was an Addictions Group starting at 10:00 so I decided to give it a try. Reluctant and cynical, I made my way through the orderly's desk and was permitted to enter the 200 ward. A lot of crying and yelling could be heard in the hallways. Sitting in this group was at first a little disconcerting. One guy kept banging a stick and interrupted every person who spoke. I kept my mouth shut as the session progressed. Once over, I went back to my room for the rest of the day.

Throughout the day and night, without knocking, an orderly or nurse would open my room's door and stick their heads in to check on me....a real invasion of privacy that angered me. The showers were not set up for those of us with disabilities. My stay here was not off to a good start. The next morning, during my daily check-ins with the doctors, I voiced my concerns...and was surprised that they were heard. Staff started knocking on my door and a shower bench was found for me.

Each day, I'd attend the Addictions Group and each day I became more comfortable with the sessions. Similar to AA, but with the added bonus of structured daily topics led by two incredible staff members. The sessions were to last 50 minutes, but if the session was going well, staff would continue on, sometimes up to a couple of hours. I learned a great deal about stressors, triggers and tools needed to help me kick my addiction. After the sessions ended, I was left on my own. After a few days, I was allowed to leave the floor four times a day for an hour each. A trip to Tim Hortons and a walk in the sunshine were welcome. You had to sign out at the orderly's station, grab your charging cords (I'd charge my stuff each time in the lobby of the hospital.) My first trip outside, what do I see? A Beer Store! Surprisingly, it didn't bother me. Just having this little bit of freedom was just what I needed. It was at this point, I knew life was about to get better.....

Part two next week. Until then, stay safe and look out for one another.....

He's Alive! The Last Chapter...

Life continued on the 7th floor of Victoria Hospital. Daily Addictions group, check-ins from the psychiatry team were the norm. Early on, I met a woman from Addiction Services who began to visit regularly. After going through an in-take session, I was encouraged to set up at a program at their Queen's St. location once I was discharged from the hospital. I was also now homeless, having been formally evicted. However, I was starting to feel really good about my future and my health. Hell, I reached rock bottom, so the only way was up, right? The psychiatric team saw great progress in my return to good health. They felt I was no longer a threat to myself and started to reward me with longer passes out of the hospital. They also insisted I stay at the hospital until I found a place to live. In the end, I was free to come and go as I needed or wanted. I was really starting to feel like the old Gerry, but somewhat new and improved.

With my diabetes in check, my drive to stay sober unquestionable, and the outlook on life improving each day, I felt a really sense that I wasn't done on earth yet. Yes, there were some days that weren't so positive. Some days, I stayed in my room, kept to myself and either continued to write my novel, and just enjoyed quiet time. Here is where I discovered that the medical teams held the power. One day, feeling very quiet, a male nurse come into my room, unannounced, and in a rather "I really don't care but its my job" manner, asked me how I was. I responded that I was having a quiet day. The next day, my doctor came to see me to ask why I was being so uncooperative? I said I was but preferred to be left alone. The doctor accepted my explanation and asked if my meds were enough. I was (and still am, on a low dose antidepressant). The doctor encouraged me to up my dose and I said no thank you. This is where I learned treatment was about pharmacology rather than counselling.

One morning, I could hear an argument taking place outside of my room. I opened a door to see the same, uncaring nurse shouting at a patient, who, during my time there, was a friendly dude. Apparently, staff had the ability to search patient's rooms when they were not present to determine if there were any prohibited items in their rooms. I can understand the premise behind this, but to do it without the patient present was a concern for me. Bad enough staff were entering our rooms without knocking, but these inspections were almost prison like. I expressed these concerns to my doctor that day.... from that moment on, staff knocked before entering.

Having a place to live taken care of, I was discharged a month after being admitted. Couldn't have felt more excited. My plan was to continue to attend AA meetings and follow through on attending Addiction Services appointments. To say I'm glad I did follow through is an understatement. The sessions were so valuable in my recovery program. The staff were non-judgemental and helpful. I waded through the processes and paperwork, with the help of my family doctor, to apply for (successfully) assistance from ODSP. I know many people who have had trouble with ODSP, but my application was quickly approved. Place to live: check. Income: check. Road to recovery: ongoing.

As the weeks went on, life was proving to me that I was lucky to be alive. I finished my first novel, enjoyed life in Old South, got a cat (he's such a jerk) and the sun continued to shine.

None of this would have happened were it not for the caring people in my life and the professionals I encountered who saved my life. And each day, I remind myself that I'm so fortunate to have people in my life who worked hard on my behalf and helped me get my life together. But I'm also proud of myself. I worked hard to recover, embraced the help that was available, swallowed my pride quite a bit and accepted that I had a long road ahead of me, but with a positive attitude and encouragement from some wonderful people (and you know who you are...Nadine, my family, Chef MC, and so many others), I will come out on the other side a much better person.

I had coffee with a great friend last week and something he said really stuck in my head. People who know me never expected this from me. No one, including those closest to me, knew the mental pain I was in...how could they? I hid it very well, so there was nothing to worry about! People would ask: "why didn't you reach out to me for help? Why didn't you reach out to the various agencies that are available to help?" Simple answer: I was too embarrassed and ashamed. I was too drunk to make the proper decision. And I didn't know where to turn. I do now. And I am grateful for the professionals and AA for picking me up off the ground, dusting me off and encouraging me in a non-judgemental way, especially the team at Addiction Services. And now, after several columns and ramblings, here is the point to telling my story.

My first column told the story of my life in Byron. I was blissfully ignorant to the goings on in the real world. I saw a drunk or an addict and I would wonder to myself, what the hell is wrong with these people that they can't kick the habit and why were they not strong enough mentally to get help. I have always been a person who tried to understand mental illness and help remove the stigma that comes with this illness. But I never really appreciated the causes and especially the connection to addiction. And, as hard as it to admit it, I really didn't care. Homelessness? Not my problem. Poverty: nope, don't care. I was too busy chasing a career and success. My ex-wife once said she felt like a single parent at times because I was too busy focusing on my career. My kids, now grown up, were always a priority for me. When I wasn't working, I was coaching or volunteering in some capacity. But I wasn't paying attention to the world around me.

These columns have been therapeutic. I'm not embarrassed about who I am today. I've been sober for well over a year and made a conscious decision to make a stronger effort to not only be a better person, but to care and try and help our neighbours and our world much more than I have. As an alcoholic, I know appreciate what those with addictions go through and maybe, I can help point anyone who asks for help in the right direction to get the assistance they need. By no means am I an expert. But knowing the system a little better, I have a responsibility to share that knowledge. It would be the same for a new amputee. I know what life was like in the beginning and the incredible struggle I went through, and if I can make it easier for just one person, I've done something right.

These writings were never, EVER, about looking for sympathy. This not a pity party. Nor are these writings meant to be boastful. The lessons I learned over the past two year are invaluable. My role on this earth is to share what I've learned and to impart that knowledge. I've become a much better person than I ever was, thanks to the helping hands of those who offered. These wonderful people are why I'm alive today and the honour of their generosity needs to be paid forward. I have committed to sharing my experiences in the hope that someone can either learn from it and be more tolerant of others, or to let people know that I understand what you may be going through and I'm here to help. As I said, I'm not an expert. I just now know where to point you should you be in need. To those suffering right now, there is hope. And there are far more people in our city that care and will help than you could imagine. You just need to reach out. As I have said many times publicly, I'm here to help.

Thank you to those who have followed this long-winded story. Future blogs to come with be (hopefully) interesting, fun at times and about life on this planet through the eyes of a one-legged pants less alcoholic dude.
Lastly, to those who cared, who never abandoned me and made me the new and improved Gerry, thank you and I love you more than you can possibly imagine.

Pantsless One Legged Old Guy

Most people in my world know that I've always joked about being pantsless. Where does this come from-why pantsless? I don't know when my anti-pants lifestyle started, probably as a kid. The farthest I can trace this back to is approximately 1987.

I was a young, 21-year-old working in the landscaping business. Obviously, the long hot days made wearing shorts the obvious choice. Young, tanned and in amazing shape, I worked 50-60 hours a week and loved every minute of it. Even in winter, I dressed down as we transitioned into snow removal. Early February was tree pruning time and again, I was dressed appropriately, and yes, wearing pants.

In May 1989, the unthinkable happened. While cutting the lawn on a hill, I slipped, and my foot went under the lawn mower. We had safety bars on the mowers, but in this business, time was of the essence and we generally tied the bar up, preventing it from shutting off.

I lay on the hill and looked down and saw the top of the shoe was missing and to my horror, so was most of my big toe. My boss, seeing this, ran to grab the truck and I was taken to St. Joe's emerg. I was seen by a plastic surgeon and taken for surgery hours later to repair the damage. Thus, began a long year of screwed up surgeries. You see, plastic surgeons generally do not work on feet. I won't get into details because they're kind of gross, but I would spend many months with my foot in the air. Sitting around an apartment, I would wear shorts.

During this time of recovery and botched surgeries, I wasn't moving or exercising much. Then it happened- I on weight When the accident happened, I was 240 pounds and in terrific shape. I ballooned a little. I would return to work and take the weight off but became very used to shorts. I hated pants. I left the business to return to university. Again, a lack of exercise and I started to put weight back on. Eating the wrong foods while I studied helped pack on the pounds.

Later, during my time at Domino's Pizza, working in in hot environments, while always wearing pants as this was a uniform requirement, I couldn't wait to get home and strip off the pants. My weight went up and down, depending on the time of year. Working at a pizza joint didn't help.

In 1999, I started a ten-year stint at Western University, a job that required the wearing of business suits. One thing I hate wearing in this world are suits-especially since pants are part of the equation. I was the operations manager for Food Services and managed a number of food courts. Food courts which served customers from a number of franchises such as Harveys, Tim Hortons, Manchu Wok and more. At this point, I was already a long-term coffee addict. I drank XL 3 sugar and 3 cream-18% cream. With free access to this wonderful selection of fast foods and multiple Tims location- well, you know what happened. I got FAT.

Figure 1: Fat Bastard (source unknown)

When I say I got fat, I mean FAT. Lack of exercise and really bad food choices helped pack on the pounds very quickly. I went from a size 36 waist all the way up to an eventual size 54. I was always hot and as soon as I got home, the suit came off and into my gigantic shorts. I shovelled snow in shorts and the cold never bothered me. I need a fan at my bedside to keep me cool.

It was in April 2004 and a co-worker, very bluntly, said I looked like hell and referred to me as "walking death." I was feeling like crap and finally went to the doctor. When they did the bloodwork, I swear to god all that came out was coffee cream! I was then told I had now had type 2 diabetes. I went home, obviously upset and embarrassed. When I walked in to my house, I found a brand-new membership card-my wife had signed me up for a gym membership. At first, I balked. There was no way this fat bastard was going to a gym. After some convincing, I went for the first time.

For those of you that have never endured the torture of a gym, I always thought that they were meat markets and I had zero interest in this type of environment. The Goodlife I joined was geared towards an older crowd. I decided to try a treadmill. I waddled my oversized ass on to the machine and my wife showed me how to use it. First, enter your weight which I did. The machine might have well said "get off the machine fat guy- you're going to break me." Apparently, there is a 350-pound weight limit. I am, embarrassingly, weighed 420. (sorry if that made you spit your coffee out all over your phone.) Yes-420 pounds.

So, feeling dejected, I lied to the damn machine and entered 350. And off I went. Damn thing nearly killed me. I sort of stayed with a regular exercise routine, gradually moving on to cross trainers and weights. A planned trip to Florida was part of the incentive to lose weight. Last thing I wanted Floridians to see a pale Canadian beached whale. I got into a routine where I would head to the gym at 5:00 a.m., dressed in shorts no matter the weather. Over a very long period of time, I got down to size 46 and was feeling much better.

My weight went up and down throughout the years that followed. Gain weight, diet for various trips to Florida, come back, eat all kinds of crap and so on. Many of you know what I'm talking about. As I moved into a new job in 2009, I managed to get down to 260 pounds and was feeling quite amazing.

In 2016, as many of you know, I got sick and got down to 165 pounds- very underweight and looking, well, like hell. Nothing like an infection to help with the ole weight loss. Since then, the infection flares up, but I manage to maintain my weight at 220 lbs and am a size 36. I was a 54......now I'm a 36. I basically lost 200 pounds. I must have eaten an average sized human somewhere along the way.

After losing the leg, the pantsless thing continued. Much easier to put shorts on over a fake leg. Putting jeans on is almost impossible. Can't count the number of times I've tried to get dressed and got stuck in my pants. Please don't try and imagine the scene-it isn't pretty (but kind of funny if I do say so myself.)

So, in the end, what started as somewhat of a joke, then turned into a necessity, I am known as the pantsless one legged old guy. I will remain pantsless for as long as I can. I am proud to be a part of the Anti-Pants Revolution.

Bottom line: I hate pants.

Suicide and Bourdain

Most of my readers know my story. On April 17th, 2017, I tried to commit suicide and almost succeeded. Thanks to my guardian angel, I'm still walking this earth annoying the hell out of people.

Most of my circle did not know that this was coming. And before I continue, this is NOT about trying to get sympathy for people. Absolutely not!! What I'm trying to illustrate is that its extremely difficult to see that someone is in so much pain that they will take their own life. Some suggest that suicide is cowardly and selfish. I suppose in my case, that may be true....or maybe its not. I am far from being an expert on this topic. I'm hoping a little insight may assist others in the future.

To illustrate my point, I want to talk about Anthony Bourdain. I am a huge fan of Bourdain's work but I would never assume to have known him. Bourdain took his own life on June 8th 2018 in a hotel room in France. He was found by his close friend Eric Ripert. Now, as many of Tony's fans, me included, when hearing this news would exclaim, "Whoa! Didn't see that coming!" To outsiders and his fans, Bourdain, we assumed, was living the dream. Popular host of "No Reservations" and "Parts Unknown", travelling the world, an opportunity most of us will never get. If you're read "Kitchen Confidential", you know it took Bourdain many years before finally making it in this world. So, the question arises, "Why, when globetrotting and making money" would Tony take his own life? We can guess and theorize all we want. At this point, we may never know. His circle didn't see it coming and you just know friends like Zamir Gotta or Eric Ripert would have done everything they possibly could.

> "Travel changes you. As you move through this life and this world you change things slightly, you leave marks behind, however small. And in return, life - and travel - leaves marks on you. Most of the time, those marks - on your body or on your heart - are beautiful. Often, though, they hurt."
> — Anthony Bourdain

I hate clichés, but "hindsight is 20/20" is true. Having watched almost every episode of Bourdain's shows, there were little hints or signs that he was suffering to the average viewer. Anthony regularly joked about killing himself or hanging himself. During an episode on Spain, apparently the country with the highest number of psychotherapy professionals in the world, Bourdain "portrayed" a mental health patient. Looking back, it may not have been the portrayal everyone thought. While watching his many episodes, it was clear Tony had very low self esteem. He implied many times he'd be going to hell and didn't practice a religion as it was hypocritical so he thought.

> "Maybe that's enlightenment enough: to know that there is no final resting place of the mind; no moment of smug clarity. Perhaps wisdom…is realizing how small I am, and unwise, and how far I have yet to go. - Anthony Bourdain"

Of course, I have a theory as to why Bourdain took his own life, but its just a theory and to share that theory would be irresponsible. I have imagined the incredible pain or depression Tony must have felt. You can't tell me that this man, who was the father of a little girl and friend to many didn't consider what the effects of his death would have on his world. I can speak from my own experience that I thought of my two amazing now adult kids constantly while planning my own death. I did think of the effects of what this act would do to my family and my beautiful Nadine. I did....it took me days to plan this out. I cried, went back and forth on whether I should take m own life. Bourdain was a heavy drinker. So was I. I was aging...and so was he. We were both in so much pain that our alcohol fueled decision making was clouded and not intelligent. But, no one, and I mean no one, knew what we were going through.

"It can happen that you lose relatives or family members and one does not feel bitter — it's life and losses happen. But then there are people who are in your life with the same sense of family and understanding and their death brings shock and collapse, as if we had a shared DNA and their death is like a death within our hearts too." Zamir Gotta

After much thought about why Bourdain took his own life, I've now turned my attention on the good he brought to this world. He taught us to live life while we're here, to get out and explore the "Parts Unknown", try different foods, even as Tony put it, it means spending hours on the "thunderdome" the next day. He told us incredible stories of resilience (check out his stories on Laos and Oman), he introduced us to Zamir Gotta, a very outgoing, warm and hilarious Russian broadcaster (Zamir appears in 10 episodes...and these episodes are the most enjoyable for me...check out his visit to Kansas City). We also met Eric Ripert, a very talented chef and a very kind soul who practices Buddhism. Ripert taught us to enjoy life but to be respectful and gentle. There is an episode in Sichuan China and Bourdain has Ripert try various local hot foods. I couldn't stop laughing. We are introduced to the wonderful and giving people of the Philippines, the drug crisis in West Virginia that is literally killing a town and the kind people of Vietnam.

"Anthony was my best friend. An exceptional human being, so inspiring & generous. One of the great storytellers who connected with so many. I pray he is at peace from the bottom of my heart." Eric Ripert

From Stats Canada:

The suicide rate for males was three times higher than the rate for females (17.9 versus 5.3 per 100,000).

Although suicide deaths affect almost all age groups, those aged 40 to 59 had the highest rates.

Again, I'm not an expert but stats show men commit suicide more often than women. Historically, older men have been taught to hide their feelings and don't show emotion. Years ago, during a crisis at work that affected our whole team at work, there was no way anyone, especially my males bosses, would see me cry. The stress at work was so incredibly heavy that I did want to cry, but waited until the car ride home. Showing emotion was a sign of weakness. So it is not surprise that men in the 40-59 age group are killing themselves. As a 52 year old man, I've grown to not care if I'm judged. I cry now. I accepted professional help and now talk about what troubles me and I now deal with the baggage I used to carry. I have learned that I still have so much to do on this earth, love to give and so many more people to piss off (I jest...maybe).

We've heard stories about the wait times in hospitals for those seeking assistance. Yes, as a society, we need to work much harder and spend the money to make access to mental health much easier. But consider that at least you're now safe....and help is coming. The people I dealt with were caring and got me back on the road to good health.

My closest and dearest friend has a philosophy that we should celebrate people while they are alive and not wait until they have passed. She is absolutely right. It is sad we didn't celebrate Bourdain while he was alive, but let's enjoy and celebrate his legacy and, as we press ahead with life, let's challenge ourselves to celebrate each other. I am asking that we do at least three things as we carry on about our life:

- Check in with the people in your world
- If a man or woman turns to you for help, listen....don't judge and be compassionate
- Celebrate each other.

I am here to help and to listen. Or check this link for help: https://www.canada.ca/en/public-health/services/suicide-prevention/warning-signs.html

Bottom line: let's look out for one another.....

Cooks, Drugs, Booze and Anthony Bourdain

Even though I've been in the food business for quite some time and I've got some game in the kitchen, I'd never consider myself a cook or a chef. Oh sure, no one can make pound lasagna like me. But the title of cook or Chef is something one earns. The Chef label, in my opinion, has been bestowed upon some individuals who have never earned the right to be called Chef even though they may have been put in charge of a kitchen. It takes thousands of hours to get a Red Seal and countless hours working in a variety of eateries to earn the right to be called Chef.

It is also my belief that many diners do not have a clue as to what goes on in a kitchen. Sure, there are movies like "Waiting" starring Ryan Reynolds that give some insight as to the goings on in the back of the house, but it doesn't come close in some scenes. The kitchen and those who toil in it, are a special group of people who, unless they're Jamie Oliver, really don't get any recognition or high reward for what they do.

Kitchen staff, like hockey goalies, are a crazy bunch of people and believe me, not everyone is cut out for the culinary racket. For some, its the path to the rise in ranks to become a Chef and then hopefully, own their own restaurant. For others, its a job that they fall in love with and decide to stay in this field. But for many, its a crappy job that many jump into in order to pay the rent. If you don't believe me about the last group, read Anthony Bourdain's "Kitchen Confidential" as it proves my point. Bourdain went through it all before jumping to the Food Network and the Travel Channel.

The kitchen teams, from the dishwashers, line cooks, sous-chef and the Chef, work some of the most ridiculous hours you can imagine. Dinner service or buffet for 400 that starts at 6:00 p.m. means the crew is in for 8-10 hours the day before prepping and

then are in at 8 or 9 the next morning and will be working straight through till 9 or 10. The kids who work the dish pit may start at 3 and work till midnight or 1:00 in the morning. Coffee and smoke breaks are sometimes few and far between and when they do get a break, you'll find most of them sitting on milk crates out back.

At the Fair, some days were almost impossible, but the kitchen seem to always pull it off. Let me give you a scenario: The first Friday in December was usually one of the craziest:

- Craft Show
- Hockey Tournament
- Dinner for 450 at the Top of the Fair
- Christmas Dinner for 400 in the Carousel Room

- Christmas Dinner for 150-200 at Yuk Yuks
- Live horse racing

All this in one day. The team would drag themselves in, work like mad in one kitchen, deliver and serve all of these patrons, go home late, come in early the next day, usually hungover, and do it all again...usually not bitching about it ether. Why? Its what they do. For very little money or praise. They get crapped on for every small mistake yet rarely are thought of, except for the Chef who gets all the accolades. Working in hot sweaty kitchens, sometimes with lousy equipment or in a very small confined space, the cooks pound out meal after meal. Whether it was an order of chicken tenders and fries (don't even mention chicken tenders to cooks) or a perfect prime rib, the care and sweat that goes into each plate is unappreciated. Imagine the board is full of chits, the grill and fryers are full and the pressure is on....the team is in the weeds. Yet, they pull it off.

"There's a bond among a kitchen staff, I think. You spend more time with your chef in the kitchen than you do with your own family." Gordon Ramsey

Many in the culinary world work until the wee hours of the morning. They stick together after hours since everything is closed and party on pay day. Drinking and drugs go hand in hand with cooking staff. Some take it a bit too far. One day, in one of my restaurants, I walked in and watched a cook chopping something on a cutting board. I looked down and there was nothing there. I asked him what he was chopping, and in his best stoner voice, he advised he was chopping onions. I told him that there were no onions on the cutting board...it was empty. I then asked if he'd been smoking up and he said "yeah, a bit" but didn't think it was an issue. The guy was totally wasted. I had to let him go. There are those who drink or use so much, they form addictions and try as hard as they can to not use at work, the usage would grow. Drinking on the job or snorting cheap cocaine was part of their day. In some cases, I didn't know this was happening and when I did know, I'd try and get them help. If you haven't watched Gordon Ramsey's expose on cocaine, you really should.

Some cooks found that cooking saved their lives and gave them purpose and actually saved their lives. Watch any episode of "Chopped" and you'll see many cooks tell the story about how they were lost and cooking saved their lives. During an episode of "No Reservations" in Washington, Bourdain profiles two ex-cons who were running a kitchen for those in need of meals. Saved their own lives and turned their worlds around.

I enjoy cooking shows like Chopped and I especially enjoy Gordon Ramsey, not the Fox TV American version but the British version featured on "The F Word" or "Kitchen Nightmares". Ramsey started the same way as most cooks, young, cocky, trouble making little assholes. But, he started taking cooking seriously and built an empire. Not every cook, hardly any, get to make it as far as Ramsey.

"I wouldn't call being a chef gratifying in a lot of ways. It's an act of love." Alex Guarnaschelli

But Anthony Bourdain is my favourite because of how many years he toiled in restaurants, the drug addiction that he managed to kick, the many years that he was broke, the success he finally achieved and, most importantly, the lessons he teaches on his shows. Yes, it was very clear he still had alcohol issues, but he seemed to persevere. His many episodes of "No Reservations" and "Parts Unknown" took us to parts of the world we never knew existed. His story telling was addictive, teaching us about the people of the world, learning about their struggles, all while enjoying their local cuisine. I will write so much more on Bourdain in the weeks to come.

And here is an important point: if you can, get to the food places you wouldn't normally think of and talk to the owners and cooks. I think you'll find some incredibly interesting stories. Chain restaurants are great and have their place. Try digging into a small independent restaurant, especially when travelling. The food is often better and the conversations are intriguing.

I do have the honour of knowing several talented and amazing Chefs. My friend, Michael Coleby, is still one of the most talented craftsman I know. His ability to create such magic for his guests in incredible. My friend Nadine has taught me so much in the kitchen....flavours, different foods and the art of cooking. She can take old leftovers from any fridge and create a masterpiece. The Springs on Springbank Dr had a very creative and talented chef. He offered foods I had never tried and I was astonished at the quality. I had a young chef at The Fair who reminded me that keeping flavours and spices simple allows you to enjoy the beauty of a dish without masking the flavour. One of my favourite restaurants, The Church Key, introduced me to foods that were new to this old guy and his boring flavours. They made me fall in love with the potato again...weird. I had a kitchen manager at The Fair, Keith B, who never claimed to be a Chef, teach me the value of a great team and the excitement that comes from a great service.

However, behind each of these talented Chefs are the line cooks, prep staff and dishwashers. The heart and soul of every successful eatery. People like Al, Pam, Luke, good ole Ronnie, Matt and Phil, Robyn, Peter, JP, Mike and Mike (yes...I had a team with a Mike and a Mike), Chong and Sue, Mihn, Deb B and many others who were the life blood of the kitchen who made the Chef and owners look like superstars. Guys like Ian in the dish pit are the real heroes, doing the hardest, filthiest and most disgusting work in the kitchen that always goes unrecognized.

The cooking game is a tough one. And very unappreciated. These men and women feed us the most delicious foods and rarely get thanked. I challenge you: The next time you dine out, ask your server if they tip out the kitchen. If they say no, maybe think of going elsewhere in the future. This is a sign that the front and management aren't giving enough appreciation to the true artists....the cooks. I'm a very experienced manager and can handle an easy kitchen that serves burgers....I could never handle a true kitchen. I'm thankful to every cook who I worked with....all I can say is WOW!

Happy Birthday Canada...Eh!

Okay all you Labatt 50 drinking hosers, my take on Canada Day.

This morning, CBC tweeted out a question: "What do you love most about Canada?" I took a second to think about it and then posted an answer: The People! I will explain why shortly....

There are so many things about this vast and beautiful country of ours that I enjoy:

- That we argue about whether its pronounced POOTINE or POU-TIN
- That we debate whether raisins belong in butter tarts. (They DO!)
- That there are thousands of Tim Hortons location across the country where I can get my much needed caffeine fix
- That even though my beloved Leafs haven't won a cup since I was in diapers, I'm still a diehard fan
- That we shut down as a country when our Canadian athletes compete for gold.
- The London Knights and The Sarnia Sting
- That when I needed emergency health care, it was there and saved my life
- My bags of milk....hate the jugs.
- That our education system helped both my now grown up kids become honour students and damn fine citizens
- Chapmans Ice Cream and what they did for their team when their plant burned to the ground
- Kitchen parties in Nova Scotia

- Signal Hill and Cabot Tower in St Johns Newfoundland where I sat and watched the icebergs go by as the sun came up
- Fresh fish and chips
- Bridge Fries in Sarnia
- Canada Day in Charlottetown PEI
- Watching the Expos in Montreal
- Camping in the Gaspe
- Ottawa...nothing more to be said
- The Behemoth at Canada's Wonderland even though I thought I was going to die
- Flying over the Rockies
- Golf in Kamloops BC
- Lake Huron
- The Muskokas
- Grecos Pizza in North Bay
- The Wortley breakfast on weekends

I could go on and on, but I won't. What is common about everything that I love about this country and specifically the list above is the people. Everywhere I have gone, the people stood out. Proud, modest, helpful and friendly. Canada is home to the greatest mix of folks in the world! I have met some incredible individuals in my 51 years and for this I am grateful and wouldn't trade this great country for anything. Here in London, I have grown to enjoy and respect the people I have met, coached with, worked with and played with...there are no better people.

I have seen strangers buy lunch for a homeless person downtown and volunteers are work tirelessly for their organizations and charities. For example, I have worked with outstanding people at The Salvation Army during the Christmas Hamper program. WOW! I see people give over and over again to the Food Bank I have met great doctors, nurses, support staff, teachers, police officers and firefighters, garbage collectors and crossing guards. I have interacted with superb staff at my favourite restaurants and coffee shops. I have watched our children grow into brilliant minds who also care a great deal about people.

I have many friends. They say you are a lucky person if you have a couple of close friends. I am extraordinarily lucky as I have had so many different friends who care a great deal about me....all selflessly being there, checking in with me, knowing the struggles I have faced in the past. I am still here on this earth thanks to these wonderful people. And you know what...they asked for nothing in return. They simply did it because they cared and are such amazing individuals. I am the person I am thanks to the great people of Canada. This makes me proud!

My point is that, yes, Canada has such a wonderful landscape, something you won't find in many places in the world. But its the people who make us who we are as a country. To steal and maybe change a little a line from the movie **Thor Ragnorok**, Canada isn't a place, its a people. Wherever we Canadians are, we are an extraordinary people who are respected and loved throughout the world.
So, Happy 151st Birthday my friends.... enjoy the day, crack open a Canadian or enjoy an Ice Capp, stay cool, shoot off some fireworks and continue to look out for each other!

Foodies- A Special Group of People

I never wanted to be a foodie. I dreamt of being a cop or a history teacher. But I guess my path in the hospitality world would be my destiny. Looking back, I'm glad I followed this accidental road in life. Food service people play a critical role in the lives of people. A screwed up coffee can piss a customer off. An amazing dinner out makes for a great evening. Food is a break for people in their daily lives. Quick story: there was a student at Western who, every Friday, would come to our Harvey's location....and he was a dick. For years he was a dick. When he graduated, he came back to the staff at our Harveys and thanked them and apologized for being such an ass. Made everyone's day!

At age 13, I got my first taste of the food services world. My mom hooked me as a busboy/dishwasher at the Legion on Oakland Ave. Cleaning dirty ashtrays, collecting empty beer bottles and glasses, stocking the bar for the bartenders. Not the most glamourous job, but hell I even met Miss Universe during one event. I'd wash dishes, help the ladies auxiliary prep and serve food. I did whatever jobs they asked, and quite happily. I was Lucy's boy, the ladies loved me and they even gave me money for it. I'd work the New Year's Eve party and then come back first thing the next morning to help with the New Year's Levee. Pretty cool. But the people I worked with were the best part.

Fast forward a few years. After university, I came home one day and my wife announced that she was losing her job, so I better go get one. There was an ad for an Assistant Manager at Domino's Pizza. Fast food? Not a chance would I lower myself to work at a fast food job. My wife explained a job was a job so I applied.....and got the job. Nervous and a little embarrassed,

I donned my new Domino's uniform and headed to the Wonderland Rd store (now relocated to Masonville). I started at 3:00 p.m. and was immediately put on the makeline and taught how to make pizzas. The night was busy, I was out of my league and hated the work. Midnight came and went and I was still at work. Finally, at about 2:00 a.m., I was allowed to go home. My wife was waiting up for me and I announced that there was no way in hell I'd go back. I lasted 5 amazing years!

I was promoted to store manager of the busiest store in London and the second busiest in Canada. (We were the second store in the country to hit a $1,000,000 in sales....a lotta dough. I also learned that our team was a group of amazing individuals. High school and university students worked inside and guys who drove part time while holding a full time job. Most of our team really cared about the business and gave it their all. Friday nights, Super Bowl and Halloween were the best...we'd get slammed and knock it out of the park. Snow storms...no problem. My guys seemed to get extra pumped up. One night one of our guys...Gord (a great and brilliant guy) headed out to his car with a pizza delivery, loaded up Guns n Roses' "Welcome to the Jungle". I knew it would be a great night! Ryan (a very loyal friend and. terrific guy) and I would have gummy bear eating contests, we'd listen to the Art Bell show late a night. We all worked an incredible amount of hours each week. These people were amazing and to this day, many of them are still my friends (surprising since I was quite the asshole at times). Our owner, Dale Hoose was and still is one of the greatest person I've ever worked with. The company is now in the hands of two amazing people, one them being my good friend Sewch and to this day I'm still loyal to the brand.

The long hours and the arrival of a new baby was taking a toll on my life. An opportunity to work at UWO came up and I was strongly encouraged to apply. I knew the guys at Western during our business interactions on the Meal Plan. I applied, didn't get the job initially, but was recruited a year later and I took the job, managing CentreSpot, the largest retail food court on campus. It broke my heart to leave Domino's but it was time to grow. A Monday to Friday day job was perfect for me and my young family. My only hesitation was working with a union. At the time, I was very anti-union. And this would never ever be a Monday-Friday day job.

In short, the union I worked with at Western were some of the most incredibly dedicated people I have ever had the honour to work with. The union made me a far better manager than I could have ever imagined. I'm not saying every employee was a model employee. That's true in every field. But the majority were absolutely phenomenal. This where I learned that a good manager listens. I had a supervisor, Susan, make a suggestion to close down one of her two food outlets and combine them into one. I didn't pay it much attention. The idea to combine the two outlets moved forward, despite my objections. In the end, Susan knew far better than I did and I was taught a valuable lesson: listen to your front line staff. They know what they are talking about!

Learn about your team and you'll be surprised. I had a woman, Wendy, who started working for us shortly after arriving from China. One day I started talking to her and learned that while in China, she was a cardiac surgeon and was trying to get her credentials in Canada. The lady serving chicken balls was a surgeon? Pretty amazing. Another time, a gentleman by the name of Mihn was brought to my attention looking for a job. I asked for a resume and he quickly scribbled one out on a piece of paper in script I couldn't understand. His friend, a great guy named Chong, talked me into hiring him. Mihn has turned out to probably be one of the most loved members of the Western Team...ever.

I also worked with an incredible support team at Lambton Hall. Janet, Margaret, Mary to name a few, were dedicated to the Western Mission. Working far more than the 40 hour work week, they made us out in the field look amazing. Both Janet and Margaret taught me what team work and dedication were all about.....and they also taught me far more than they'll ever know!

And Western is where I met the great Chef Michael....a man who would become a very close friend. Everything I ever learned about catering and food came from Michael and his team. I would later take what I learned from Michael and use it as the benchmark for what I expected out of chefs I would work with in the future.

There are far too many Western foodies to name, but people like Lisa, Daisy and Salwa, Union Prez Cindy, JP, Denise (god rest her soul), Danica and Angie, Chong and Sue, Dave, Mirza (who always spoiled my kids), Peckham (you know who you are),Simon and Jenn, Matt and Sue are some of the greatest people I have ever worked with. Their passion for outstanding service in an incredibly demanding environment makes Western's Hospitality Services one of the tops in the country! These fine folks would work their 40 hours then volunteer to work in the cold rain at TD Waterhouse Stadium feeding thousands of homecoming fans. The positive impact that these outstanding people make in the lives of staff, alumni and students is immeasurable.

I moved on to Compass Group Canada. Again, proving I'm a complete idiot and don't know what I'm talking about, I thought contract companies were all about the bottom line and screwing over the customer. I was hired into the Leisure Division and learned I was so bloody wrong .....again! I received more training and education than I thought possible, most of it focused on our people. I was assigned to the SSEC (RBC) Centre, home of the Sarnia Sting....and it was expected that I would act like I was the owner....how would I run the food services department if I owned it? This philosophy was important not only in the financial management of the business, but in the human resources side. I met a passionate bunch of people who had worked at the arena for years....not only my team, but the arena team as well. It takes a whole team to put on an OHL game and I was so impressed with this wonderful group of people. The Atmores, Mike the Chef, Vicky, Chantal (the hash slinger), Mabby (coolest Zamboni driver....ever), Trevor who ran the facilities team, Marla the office manager, Cindy in the box office and Paul & Paula in sales are just a few of the many who make the arena such a great place to work at!

While managing the food in Sarnia, I was asked to manage the food services at the Western Fair....a huge task to say the least. An impressive operation that seems to be busy 24 hours a day. Seventeen hour work days were not uncommon and this group of superhuman individuals seem to pull it off every single event. This team provided food for shows and events, catering, racing, the hockey arena, the Fall Fair and so much more. One week we'd provide food for 1500 people in the Agriplex (no small feat I can tell you) and then provide food and beverage service for an MMA event. And rarely did I hear anyone complain. Service with a smile was the norm. Ronnie, KB, Brittany and Laura, Tiffany, Ilona, Hayatt and Samarr,

Nadine, Brodie and so many others worked until their legs were ready to fall off to provide the best customer experience....every....single....day!

Another quick story: We were looking for a sous chef. I was exhausted and busy, but was asked to meet a candidate. A woman sat before me with her portfolio. I wanted to approve the successful candidate, but I was working 80 hour weeks, so I didn't really put my full attention into the interview. This woman had a great resume, but I didn't really care at this point. I said go ahead, hire her...didn't care. Well, again, proving what a dipshit I can be, this woman went on to become the first ever female Executive Chef at The Fair. Her food was impressive, but it was her ability to put together and motivate a great team is what got her the job. She worked as many hours on her guys, worked the dish pit when needed, cheered them on each and everyday....best....hire....ever!

The success of the foodie team at the Fair was dependant on the back breaking team work of the Fair staff. Justin, Lummer, Sarah, Voytek, Kris, and their teams of unsung heroes made us look good. There is a ton of work, set up and prep that goes into every event and service that many don't know about. We couldn't have pulled any of it off if we didn't have such a great model of teamwork.

The dedication of a good foodie team isn't just limited to London or Sarnia. During my seven years with Compass, I was called upon to support many events in many different cities. At the G20 Summit in Toronto in 2010, we were tasked with serving thousands of meals each day during a two week period. Food was prepared and then shipped via truck to a variety of locations in Toronto. This is where I met the great Chef Tina who was based out of Hamilton. Tina left the family at home and worked a ridiculous amount of hours preparing this food, all with the highest quality...and with a giant smile on her face. I worked with some crazy, fun, hard working people in Toronto, Hamilton, Ottawa, Guelph, Chatham, Waterloo and Kitchener. And in every single place I went, I worked with some of the finest people you could imagine. Kirk, Tina, Kari and many others shared the same vision...dedication, outstanding food, friendliness and cooperation were the basic tools we all use.

The success at every place I worked had very little to do with me as the manager. It had everything to do with the teams I worked with each and everyday. I'm not saying every member of our team was great. There were some awful employees....and they wouldn't last long. Anthony Bourdain puts it best: **"Skills can be taught. Character you either have or you don't have."** It takes s special kind of person, with a little craziness mixed in, to work in the food business. From a high end restaurant, to a food truck or a diner, special people are making it happen everyday. In every kitchen, there is a cook, who has been online for 11 hours already, bent over a hot grill or steam table for hours on end making sure your steak is cooking perfectly (stop ordering well done!) and the plating is stunning. Every kitchen has that young person slaving in the dish pit. They all have knife scars and burn marks and they wear them like tattoos, a sign of honour. Every restaurant has a server who is working two jobs because either they are supporting a family or they just love the work. Bottom line: be nice to the foodie who serves you. They do value your business and they are working long and hard to ensure you have a good day. And no....we don't spit on your food or believe in the "5 second rule".... so there!

Lessons I've Learned from Anthony Bourdain

As CNN is set to broadcast Anthony Bourdain's last episodes of "Parts Unknown", my thoughts turn to Tony's impact on this world. When we all leave this earth, we'd like to hope we've left a positive impact on our world. I don't think many consciously think about what kind of legacy we leave behind. Oh sure, we'd like to hope many think of us as great moms and dads or an awesome friend, but I'm hoping we think much bigger. What good did we do for this world? We're we a kind person in our community.... we're we charitable....and did we pass away still learning and loving this planet? Lastly, did we make sure, while we live, that we enjoy life to it's fullest?

Bourdain left one hell of a legacy for all of us. Many lessons were learned, especially for this 52-year-old Canadian old guy. I've been in the food and beverage business for 30 years. I personally know the struggles "foodies" face on a daily basis and the toll it does on your body and soul. Tony lived this as well, and I believe that is ultimately why many of us feel connected to him. Yes, we've mourned the deaths of many "celebrities", but Tony never acted like a celebrity.... ever. He seemed like an everyday kind of dude, one we all wanted to be friends with.

I wanted to write about what impact Anthony made not only on me, but his friends and the rest of the world. I learned a lot from Bourdain and now challenge myself to use what I've discovered to make a better impact on my community. We are not on this earth to take, we are supposed to be giving. I can think of no other personality that made a greater contribution to this planet than Tony and he gave us such an incredible gift. And I have discovered, I'm not alone in that thinking. Having said all of this, here is my perspective on how much greater this world is thanks to Tony.

Lesson #1: Be generous and hospitable. The World, as big as it is, is now a worldwide community thanks to Anthony Bourdain. Tony introduced us to a world many of us didn't even know existed and to people…. really great people! It was through his shows that we were introduced to the amazing Zamir Gotta. Zamir, very close friends with Tony for many years, learned, as I did, that we are part of a global community, a realization Zamir refers to in a piece with **The Hollywood Reporter** in June 2018. This quote from Zamir is so true:

"I was fortunate to find in this life a true comrade-in-arms who, through his example, helped me throw off the chains of being Soviet born and brought up; who helped me become a citizen of the world."

Citizens of the world taught us to be welcoming, generous and hospitable. But we were also reminded of the horrors people of the world have faced. During an episode of "No Reservations" in Laos, we were introduced to a family who demonstrated how we could all behave. During the secret war in Laos during the 60's and 70's, American forces dropped more than 200 million tons of ordinance on the country. Millions of these bombs did not explode. The Laotian people have for decades toiled to find and remove these bombs. Thousands have died and many more have been maimed. (legaciesofwar.org/about-laos/secret-war-laos/).

Tony introduced us to a very poor family who have been sadly impacted by these bombs. A father, missing an arm and a leg, and his family invited Anthony to a meal...a meal provided by a family who had very little to offer. Tony graciously sat with the family and learned about the devastating impact the secret war had on them. He enjoyed a dinner offered by a family with very little means, yet their generosity shone brightly that day. In many other episodes, Anthony brings of to the dinner table of many impoverished people who time and time again show what incredible kindness and hospitable people are. Tony also highlighted the devastation Laos has faced.... maybe its a good reminder to lobby the world to help clean up the mess that Laotians are desperately trying to clean up...one bomb at a time.

Lesson learned: no matter how tough we think life is, be kind and generous!

Lesson #2: Respect!
I hate the world "tolerance". Tony taught us to learn about people and the world and to **respect** their traditions, understand their cultures and to appreciate what everyone brings to our community. When sitting down to eat with a local, you can see Anthony hesitate before eating and drinking, learning how to proceed before diving in. He didn't want to disrespect their traditions.

Bourdain took us to Iran and showed us an incredibly pleasant and generous group of people. He travelled to Manilla, where families are broken up as hard-working family members travel to other parts of the world just to get work…. often times leaving their children behind but needed to do so in order to support their family. Anthony shattered a lot of stereotypes about what we may think of people. At the beginning of an episode in Houston, Anthony opens by saying" **Prejudicial, close minded, quick to make assumptions about places that are different from where we grew up".** For example, as a Canadian, when I think of Texas, I think of cowboys, wide open country, proud Americans, beef, oil and guns. During his trip to Houston, Bourdain highlighted a huge Indian community that was helping transform the city. One segment showed a grocery store where the Indian staff would stop, dressed in traditional garb, and sing and dance Bollywood style. I couldn't stop smiling….and bloody well enjoyed this episode. I want to go there just to see this! Anthony admits, like many of us do, that he was wrong about the people of Texas.

Lesson learned: think and learn before forming opinions about people. You will learn so much and hopefully respect all peoples and traditions.

Lesson #3: Live Life!

"Life should not be a journey to the grave with the intention of arriving safely in a pretty and well-preserved body, but rather to skid in broadside in a cloud of smoke, thoroughly used up, totally worn out, and loudly proclaiming "Wow! What a Ride!" -Hunter S. Thompson

Bourdain may have said it even better: **"your body is not a temple, it's an amusement park. Enjoy the ride."** And he's right! Enjoy some street meat, try foods you've never even considered trying, meet new people, listen to different music, experience different cultures.

One of my favourite scenes in all of Anthony's shows took place in Uzbekistan. My description couldn't come close to describing what took place. Here is how Zamir Gotta tells the story during his interview with The Hollywood Reporter:

"And then there is the episode in Uzbekistan, which has gone down in history as one of the most popular among Tony's fans. "It was the very last day and we managed to secure access to the older banya [steam sauna] in town, where the local masseur was rather disgruntled about being exposed on American TV. But I paid ahead of time and the masseur then outdid himself in enthusiasm, really overdoing it in his efforts to impress Tony and me. Afterwards Tony was in agony and distress — almost as if he had undergone some kind of sexual harassment...and he knew whom to blame. But, bless him, he never once pointed the finger at me and the episode became a huge hit."

I couldn't stop laughing. Anthony would try almost anything, and his personality was contagious. An episode in Kansas City has such a fun moment involving Bourdain and Gotta. They're in the parking lot of Arrowhead Stadium, tailgating with fans. Zamir shows up dressed in every piece of Kansas City Chief's gear, jacket, toque and a giant "we're number one" foam finger and dives right into the festivities. A perfect reminder to stop being so conservative, jump in and have some fun!

Thanks to Tony, we've been introduced to people like Zamir Gotta, Eric Ripert, and Jose Andres, each with their own unique personalities who taught us to be respectful, out-going, friendly and to be kind. Andres, during one show, spoke about the simplicity of ingredients and you could see his passion. We met Nari Kye, a member of Anthony's team, who has this incredible energy and excitement that was showcased during a trip to Korea. For this, we should be thankful!

Lesson learned: Have fun, meet new and spectacular people, try new things and simply enjoy what life has to offer.

Lesson #4: Pursue your dreams and inspire people like Tony has managed to do. Bourdain may be one of the greatest story tellers. Listening to him as he narrates each of his episodes, Tony manages to paint an imaginative picture that allows viewers to completely understand what Tony sees and hears while on location. We might not have been there on location in person, but the way Anthony tells the tale, you feel like you were there.

As a 51-year-old, I found myself wanting to finally pursue my dream......writing. Listening to Tony and reading his books, inspired me to not only continue to write, but to be a better story teller. **Last week, I published my first book! Lesson learned: pursue your dreams. There is nothing stopping you.... there are no excuses!**

Lesson #5: "Its not all about me" There is nothing that drives me absolutely bonkers like when an interviewer takes over the interview, trying to prove how smart they are compared to the guest. Bourdain let the people in his shows be the star. He never interrupted a guest and let them either tell their stories or describe the food they were proud to serve

Tony. Anthony appeared to be an incredibly well spoken and well-read man but was never so arrogant to prove his brilliance. He'd always ask a cook the dish was, allowing them to describe the dish and the flavours the diner could expect. **Lesson learned: close your mouth and open your ears...you'll learn so much more.**

Lesson #6: Get off the beaten path. When I think of where I want to travel to some of the great countries of the world, obviously I think of the usual tourist destinations. I think of France, I'm going to Paris. Spain.... heading to Madrid. Watching "Parts Unknown" that our world is so much more than the tourist traps. So now I want to go to Granada instead of Madrid and try some of the fabulous Tapas the city has to offer. I'd love to head to Singapore, an incredibly clean and safe country. My plastic surgeon, who has worked his magic over the last year saving my remaining foot, travels home to Singapore quite often and says its even more spectacular than you can imagine. I never ever thought I'd want to check out Nashville, now I can't wait to check out their cuisine that I heard some many great things about.
Anthony also reminded us that our own backyards are places we need to explore. During an episode in Queens NY, Tony discovers neighbourhoods and foods from so many different cultures that you could tell he was so surprised that this all existed...just across the river.... from where he lived. Here in London Canada, we have some of the most amazing bistros, cafes and diners, but you have to go find them. I'm not suggesting stay away from the big chains, but if we would take chances, look for the little places and try foods we never imagined we'd eat. There is a place in the Wortley Village here in London called "Mai's Cafe and Bistro" where they serve some of the most incredibly tasty Thai food. The other night, I looked into the kitchen to see five tiny Thai women cooking

away.... all with smiles on their faces. So, get out there.... its a magical experience.... I promise. Most importantly, get to know the people behind the food.

Lesson learned: Explore, experiment, look past the touristy places, taste foods that are unusual; and try the places that are the "Parts Unknown."

Last lesson: Talk to someone. I can only speak from my own experience, but I didn't talk to anyone about my personal pain. I committed suicide instead. Thankfully, I survived. It turns out that, somehow, I learned that I still have so much to give to my family, friends and this world. I am proud of the direction I am going in. If you're in pain, talk to someone. If no one is there for you...**I am!!!** I can be found on Facebook or Twitter or via email at glahay1@gmail.com. I am not a professional, but I can point you in the right direction or just simply listen. You're never alone!

Some thoughts from a couple of tweets I read:

@nadezhdajohn1 writes: "Gave cooks a place of honour, proud to be in the same boat as him."

@donlemon from CNN: "If you want to honor the life of Anthony Bourdain, do what he would have done: eat something delicious, something weird ... listen to some great music, really loud. Hang out with some old friends or make some new ones. And tell your stories."

@zamirgotta: "People, good morning! We got 2 be strong....let us look out for one another. Let us celebrate people like Tony who gave us so much inspiration"

In the end, we mourn Anthony's loss. But he left us with one hell of a legacy. He taught us to be kind, respectful, to listen and learn, to celebrate life and to take risk. Through Tony and television, we became friends with the amazing Zamir Gotta who, as he has shown many times in his episodes, live life, smile and laugh, meet new people and, even at this stage in our lives, pursue our dreams. Eric Ripert taught us about kindness and patience.

So, I say to Anthony Bourdain: Thank you. You have impacted our lives in such a fantastic way. You are respected and loved and made us ask ourselves; "Will we leave such an incredible impact on this world?" If the answer is no, then maybe this is a great time to re-focus our energies.

As Zamir Gotta ended his interview with The Hollywood Reporter, he simply said this: **"As we say in Russian vechnaya pamyat —everlasting memory. Rest in peace Tony."**
Be well and happy my friends. Its a sunny day.... life is good and its up to us to make it better!

A 70's and 80's Kid

> **"Life moves pretty fast. If you don't stop and look around once in a while, you could miss it."- Ferris Bueller**

With these writings, and I suppose, as I get older, I'm turning into one of those old dudes who is starting to reminisce about life. As a kid, you'd hear "old folks" talk about the good old days and we'd wish they'd either end their story or go away because the **Bugs Bunny Roadrunner Hour** was coming on the TV in five minutes. Nothing took precedence over Bugs, Foghorn or Wile E. Coyote. But, here I am at age 52 looking back. I have to say I've been smiling a lot lately.

My childhood was not the worst, nor was it the best. My best memories came from TV, movies and music and to say they had an impact on me is an understatement.... yes.... I'm stuck in the 80's. It took until the early 2000s before I actually quit trying to maintain 80's hair.

Born in Oakville Ontario, Saturday morning cartoons were the best. **Superfriends** were a staple (although I never did like the Wonder Twins). There were the **Jetsons, Captain Caveman** and the somewhat silly **Grape Ape**. As I got older, I discovered the Hilarious House of Frightenstein starring Billy Van....a show that sort of freaked me out.... even to this day.

Then there was the transition to night time TV. There was **Kolchak: The Night Stalker** (as a kid what the hell was I doing watching this stuff?), **Charlie's Angels, The Six Million Dollar Man, SWAT, Adam 12 and one of my favourites; Emergency!** My favourite toy as a kid was the

Six Million Dollar Man with the bionic grip and the bionic eye!

My mother watched all of the soaps so I'm not stranger to **All My Children** and **General Hospital**. Then along came **The Love Boat, Fantasy Island** and **Battle of the Network Stars.** All cheesy shows but we watched them religiously. There were **Happy Days** and **Laverne & Shirley** and the show with the best theme song, **Barney Miller**. And then there was Godzilla movies. Used to watch them religiously. One night, after watching Godzilla, my mother started chasing us around the house.... until I ran headfirst into the dresser...hence the scar on my forehead! **Batman, Superman** and **Star Trek** were still popular as re-runs and I loved them all. As kids, we were also the human remote control.... flipping the dial for our parents until they decided what to watch.

The 70's brought us some great music. **Frampton Comes Alive, Elton John, ELO** and **Kiss**, were some of the first musicians I remember listening to on the radio. Although I really didn't care for **The Bee Gees** (what a mistake......there is nothing better than walking down the street strutting to Staying Alive....I'll leave that image in your head for a while), but I didn't mind disco. Heck, I even had the Pepsi Platform shoes and the coveralls to match. And yes, **Rod Stewart**, I did think I was Sexy!

Excellent coveralls and a cute dude.

This was a time when we rode our bikes for hours, played chase and dinky cars, sucked on Lolas (anyone remember Lolas?) as well as eating Lik 'Em Aid and Mojos. Pepsi introduced a new glass bottle format that was in the shape of a torpedo and if you dropped it, the bottle exploded.... good times. Hostess experimented with grape, apple and orange potato chips and they were disgusting. We read MAD Magazine and every comic book we could get our hands on. We stayed out playing until the street lights came on or your mom flashed the porch light. I delivered newspapers for the Oakville Journal Record, saw the Blue Jays play many times and sadly grew up on The Montreal Canadians as my godfather, who babysat us regularly, watched the games in French. 1050 Chum out of Toronto was the radio station of the time, playing all the greatest new hits of the time. And there was no such thing as this Inter Web everyone talks about these days.

And then......1977 happened. The greatest event, in my mind to ever hit this world. **"STAR WARS"** came out and it would forever change my destiny. Never had I seen such a fantastic story and to this day, I'm still a huge fan and, as a side note of outstanding parenting, so is my son. I still have boxes of the original toys and VHS tapes.... before they re-released them

and screwed things up.

This was also the year I moved to London Ontario. The big city when compared to Oakville. First memory was this huge White Oaks Mall. I'd never seen such a thing. A city with a population of approximately 250,000 compared to Oakville's 67,000. There were more than the two bus routes we had in Oakville. And the weirdest thing I remember were the yellow fire trucks. Being an independent 11-year-old, I explored the downtown. I discovered the giant Simpsons store, The Mascot and Medallion restaurants, the Century theatre and so much more. Downtown was the place to be (and will be again!). Zellers was everywhere, selling the best grilled cheese and fries at The Skillet. Donuts at Tim Hortons seem to be so much bigger than today.

1980: **Empire Strikes Back,** the greatest Star Wars movie ever, came out and I started high school at CCH. Armed with my big 80's hair and new Adidas gym bag, I entered the magical world of being a teenager. I also found out that the fries and gravy at Hi Lunch were the greatest thing since the invention of bologna. I'd hit the Silver Palace Arcade on Clarence St during my lunch time, pocket full of quarters, racing to master Star Gate and Space Invaders. The place would be rocking with the latest rock, **Stones, Rush, Led Zeppelin** and **The Who** and you never wanted to leave. Then the mad dash back to school for classes and football practice.

TV was changing. Comedies became the norm and for a while, they were good. **Night Court** (remember Dan Fielding?), **Mork & Mindy** and **Cheers** (which I never liked) ruled TV but nothing was more unstoppable than **The Cosby Show**. (Very disturbing what Cosby has turned into.... I used to love the guy.... Fat Albert and his stand up were terrific. Now I despise him). **Miami Vice**.......what a show. I even tried to mirror the image of a young Don Johnson, pastels, unshaven and sockless Huaraches sandals. But the music of the 80's was the bomb.... can an old guy say that?

Prince, Madonna, Robert Palmer, Simple Minds, Duran Duran and so many others ruled the radio station 1410 CKSL. **The Boss's Born in the USA** is still one of my favourite albums to this day and this was my first big time concert I'd ever seen. I had to line up all day and night at Sam's on Dundas just to get tickets to this concert. Then there was **Michael Jackson** and the Moonwalk......wow. We all rushed off to the next video stores to rent a VCR and the latest VHS tapes.... especially the Thriller video. To this day, I could listen to "Lets Go Crazy" by **Prince** over and over....and over.

The first CD I ever bought was "Brothers in Arms" by **Dire Straits**. I started buying CDs like crazy, even though I owned most of this music on albums or cassettes. I had a cheap cassette player I bought at Consumers Distributing that I smashed the first week while riding my bike on the Highbury

overpass......I worked a lot of hours at the Esso station for that damn thing.

Star Wars, Star Trek....Star Wars, Star Trek......and repeat. These were my favourite movies.... ever. Oh sure, we had **Top Gun, The Breakfast Club, Ferris Bueller's Day Off, Footloose, Beetlejuice, Caddyshack** and so many more. We cheered on Daniel in the **Karate Kid** and traveled through time with Doc and Marty in **Back to the Future**. I've seen them all countless times, but the Wars/Trek movies kept me enthralled. **Wrath of Khan** still ranks in the top 10 movies of all time. I lined up at The Park Theatre to see **Return of the Jedi** and all the **Indiana Jones** movies. The new **Batman** movies were huge (in my best Michael Keaton voice: "I'm Batman") and **Dirty Harry** made an 80's appearance with the infamous line "Go ahead. Make my day" in **Sudden Impact.**

During my late high school and adult life, I discovered Jimmy's Corners, The Oxbox, The Wellington......and beer. Summers were spent at the beach at Grand Bend, drinking Schooner beer, getting sunburnt, rocking out to **Bon Jovi, Billy Idol, Bryan Adams and Def Leppard** while working summer jobs. I once got kicked out of Fluffy's Pizza on Highbury for being......ummmm...very drunk.

The Oxbox

I worked at the Quick Lube/Esso at Adelaide and Huron and I remember listening to the Jays win their first division title then go on to lose to Kansas City......Gramma was so mad she was throwing towels at the TV! My boss at the Esso station would drop by every Sunday morning with the warmest and tastiest buns from the Portuguese bakery on Adelaide St. This is the time when KFC was actually Kentucky Fried Chicken with the giant bucket on their sign.

Saturday Night Live was hilarious. Here we were introduced to **Chevy Chase** (Christmas Vacation is still one of the must watches each year), **Eddie Murphy** (James Brown's Celebrity Hot Tub), we pumped up with **Hans and Franz**, the great Phil Hartman and so many others. **Uncle Buck** hit the big screen reminding us that **John Candy** was such a great Canadian treasure.

The amazing John Candy

I miss the 70's and 80's. They were fun times filled with great music, TV and movies. I will always smile when I look back. So many memories of a couple of great decades. I'm older now......much older and am now watching my kids grow into great adults. I hope they can look back at their youth with the same happiness that I do. My friend Michael Coleby says that "There is no future in the past." Its true.... but its a lot of fun to reminisce.

So, "May the Force Be With You" or "Live Long and Prosper"...whichever you prefer....... now get the hell off my lawn.

Dadhood- Part One

I prefer the name Dad over Father....therefore Dadhood is now an official word. Cuz I said so....

I was raised by a single mother of four. My mother worked at her full-time job and did the best she could. It wasn't the best childhood however, I turned out pretty good. As a teenager, and many of us are guilty of this, I swore I'd raise my kids differently. I also wanted to raise a whole hockey team of kids.... because parenting is easy.... (insert "you're a dumbass" joke here).

I am the very proud dad of two kids, both of whom are now in university. My kids are great students, caring citizens and spectacular athletes. But it sure as heck wasn't easy. Even as I got married, I wanted a lot of kids. My grandparents had eight kids and I wanted the same. My childhood memories of Gramma and Poppa and all of my aunts and uncles were, for the most part, amazing. This was what I wanted to re-create.

** this next little section may be a little weird......you've been warned.**

It took my wife and I a few years to conceive. We thought there was something wrong and the easiest thing to do first is to test the male. So, very begrudgingly, I trudged off to the doctor. I advised him of the concern and he brought in a nurse who would direct me to a room where I was to provide a sample. I could feel my face become beet red, but off I went to "get a sample". I was advised to put the sample in a cup and then place in a brown bag and return it to the nurse at the desk. I did as I was told, and a different staff member was at the desk. In a crowded waiting room, she yelled out "WHERE DO WE

PUT THE SEMEN SAMPLES AGAIN?" So now a room of people now knew what I was up to. In the end, my "boys" were a little slow and lazy and we just needed to be patient.

Finally, my wife announced we would be having a baby. So bloody excited, I immediately registered for Dad Classes being offered at St. Joes. The classes weren't about how to change a diaper, but rather to teach/remind dads what our responsibilities were as a dad. Dr. Campbell talked about high divorce rates and how many deadbeat dads there were out there. We were reminded that even if mom is breastfeeding, we as dads still needed to get our butts out of bed, change the diaper and burp the baby afterwards. We also attended prenatal classes...I was very capable of doing Kegel exercises by the end that I became a master. I read "What to Expect When Expecting" cover to cover. I was ready.... bring it on.

When my first child was born, I weighed significantly more than I do now. Being that my wife would be undergoing a C-section, I had to gown up. Since I was so big, I had to wear two gowns, both with some sort of rubber lining. Its August...and hot...and I was a big man. Do the math. We had no idea as to the sex of the child since there we no such thing as the gender reveal parties we see today. Minutes into the C-section, my daughter was born and was she ever a screamer. I helped with the first diaper change (bloody disgusting for a guy who gets nauseous throwing out leftovers). As I was holding the baby, I started to overheat. I said I needed to leave, and they said go ahead, take the baby with you. I went into the hall, still gowned, holding a screaming baby. I was now soaking wet and about to pass out. A staff member finally came along and helped me get out of the gowns....my shorts and t-shirt were absolutely drenched.

My daughter screamed until approximately November. Suffering from Colic, she was very uncomfortable, wouldn't eat properly and slept very little. I was working insane hours and the bulk of the parenting fell on my wife. I did what I could, but this whole father thing wasn't working for me. And I swore there would be no more kids. Six months into parenting, my wife was to return t work. She handed me the baby and said she was going out for an hour. The hour turned into a few hours. The baby wouldn't stop crying, no matter what I did. My wife returned home, and I was frazzled. She said, "now you know what its like". Lesson learned.

I mentioned I have a sensitive stomach. Changing diapers required me to suit up.... covering my face with a towel and sunglasses (so I wouldn't see the poop) and trying with all my might to not throw up on this helpless kid. I grew to enjoy this dad thing, especially when feeding time came along. Baby desserts, especially custard is amazing....one for you....one for daddy. No wonder the poor girl wasn't gaining weight.

Now, for the first terrifying moment of parenting. One night, returning home in the middle of the night from work, I found my frazzled wife was up with my daughter who was very sick. Sarah wouldn't stop throwing up, no matter what we did. I stayed up all night while my wife got a couple of hours sleep before work. We ended up taking Sarah to the hospital. It was just a bug, but she was now dehydrated. Welcome to Pedialyte. What was odd about this whole incident was that this was when Sarah became toilet trained. Now, a lesson was learned here. Pullups, the new type of underpants diaper used during training, don't come with instructions. My daughter had a poop. I again suited up and very carefully tried to pull the pullup down without losing any poop. I failed. Poop everywhere. I was retching. My wife came into the room and saw what was going on and burst out laughing. Apparently, the sides of the pullup can be torn and treated like a diaper. I had already perfected the scoop and tuck, so I would never see the poop, but NO ONE TOLD ME HOW TO USE PULLUPS.

It was decided that, since we had a huge backyard, we should buy a swing set......that I would have to put together. Now, for anyone who has ever put together a BBQ, and you know what I mean, a swing set is so much more.... ummmm......challenging. I used to be a very impatient person. So, after several days and an incredible use of every swear word known to man, I finally got the damn thing built. This kid better like this.... thankfully she did.

Sarah was an adorable curly haired little beauty. Walking around with her trusted blankey, she would sing and brought so much joy to out world. There were many times of panic as a parent and this is unavoidable. Once, I went outside for a quick second and found the door was locked. You try explaining to a toddler how to open a locked door. Grabbing the ladder, I hiked myself up the ladder, into the open bathroom window and slithered my way, head first into the window, unto the toilet and made it in. My daughter thought it was hilarious......little girl jerk.

Its my belief that every Canadian dad should build an outdoor ice rink. I thought it's be easy. Problem I failed to recognize is that my backyard was on a slope. I built the frame, put down the tarp, connected the hose to the tap in the downstairs laundry room and proceeded. A few minutes later, little toddler Sarah opened the door and said, "come quick daddy, mommy is hurt." I ran downstairs to find water on the floor...I hadn't connected the hose properly. Mommy slipped and broke her wrist. This was my last attempt at a backyard rink.

(Mommy was fine in the end...slight break.... took it like a trooper.)

My wife suggested we have another child and we discussed the pros and cons at length. I was against this...I didn't want any more kids and I was enjoying spoiling my daughter. Anyways, weeks later, I discovered we were expecting another baby. I was hoping for a little sister for Sarah. Again, via C-section and on not so hot a day, a lighter version of me dawned the gown and into the operating room we went. The doctor, after a few minutes, announced that we had a boy. I said are you sure, and he turned and handed the baby to me, and as any typical man would say, I blurted out that he was so well hung. The room laughed and off I went to help the nurse clean up my son. Phillip was born, had a huge crap, looked for something to eat and had a nap.

Phillip was a completely different baby, quiet, a good sleeper and hungry as can be. However, we decided this would be our last child. I had an appointment to get a vasectomy, again as its much easier and less invasive for the man that for a woman. For those unaware, a vasectomy is quite a simple procedure, but the doctor recommended I take some Valium before the procedure. My wife dropped me off and in I went. She would pick me up afterwards. She had some friends over to meet the new baby. Remember...I'm kind of stoned on Valium...and....much to my wife's horror, I was proud of my vasectomy and wanted to show it off, so I started to undress. I was quickly hustled off to bed. The doctors advised me to protect the area and take it a little easy. I went to work the next day as I felt I was okay. I was fine...until I got home, and my toddler daughter ran head first into my crotch......parenting is great.

I am guilty of the odd bad parenting move. One time, when my daughter was young, about five or six, she returned from the bathroom after supposedly brushing her teeth. I asked if she had really brushed her teeth to which she replied she had. I told her I had a friend at the police department who could check her toothbrush. She started to cry, and I felt like the worst dad in the world. I ended up hugging her for awhile to get her to calm down. Not my finest moment.

As a dad, I survived Teletubbies, Blue's Clues, Barney (I hate that guy), Big Comfy Couch (Damn she was annoying), Dora the Explorer (even more annoying), Arthur, and the worst of all, Hannah Montana. I built the world's worst dollhouse (stupid thing was so heavy my daughter couldn't move it). I've climbed up on the roof to retrieve balls, frisbees and a remote-control helicopter.

Sorry to break it to my kids, but I was the Easter Bunny and the Tooth Fairy. I was Santa and yes, I would spend time outside on Christmas Eve, making pretend reindeer paw prints in the snow. I ate the treats you left and drank many litres of warm milk. I was also the one who made the cool lunches you took to school.

As the kids got older, what to do with them in summer was a challenge. Working at Western, I enrolled them in Sport Western, a day long camp that had a variety of activities to engage the kids. It was such a treat to see my kids at lunch, with their little backpacks and carrying trays with their lunch. When it was time for them to go back to camp, my daughter didn't want to leave daddy, but my son was good to go and was gone in a blink of an eye.

Stuff happens to kids, usually when I was out of town. I was in Vegas one time, attending a conference. Well, there was a conference in there somewhere, in between the drinking and gambling. Slightly inebriated, I called home to see how things were. My wife was a tad cranky. Apparently, my son, while at school, managed to get a plastic bead stuck up his nose. A trip to emergency was required. As my wife described it: In order to dislodge the bead, they closed his one nostril, blew air into his mouth and the bead shot out across the room. Now, I'm slightly drunk and have this mental image in my head. I guess bursting out laughing probably wasn't the best reaction. All I heard was the clicking of the phone as she hung up the phone.

Kids and home repair projects. With kids, I was always painting their rooms or building something. When Sarah was about 5 years old, I was tasked with painting her room. This required removing about eight layers of wallpaper that the previous owner had left behind. This was a ton of work, but I was up to the task as it turns about I have a knack for it. I'm working away, listening to music when it was time for a break. Seems Sarah wanted to be a little helper and was slowly removing wallpaper in the hallway. I then knew what the next project was going to be.

I spoke about when my daughter was sick, but there was a moment where sheer terror came over me. To back up a bit, I was the Chair at the kids Parent Teacher Council. The school playground needed to be replaced and the council was tasked with raising funds. Our parents worked tirelessly to raise the $30,000 needed. We helped design a fully accessible playground, ensuring ALL kids could play on the new equipment. We helped build the new playground and finally the day came when the kids could play on the new toys.

Shortly after opening the playground for the new school year, I got a call from my wife that our son had broken his arm. I immediately became scared, jumped in my car and, breaking every traffic law possible, I made it to the hospital in record time. I arrived before my wife and son and paced nervously until they arrived. Finally, the pulled up. I whipped open the back door and my six-year-old son sat there, a few tears in his eyes. He showed me his arm to reveal a "fork fracture." I held back the tears and rushed into the children's emerg. The staff brought us into the treatment room immediately and the chief of kid's emergency medicine happened to be on duty. After an x-ray and examination, the doctor indicated that this was a common injury among kids and was an easy fix. It would require my son being asleep while they worked on fixing his arm. They stated it would not ne a good idea for us to stay as this wasn't something we would want to see. They administered an anesthetic and I watch my son go to sleep. My wife grabbed me by the arm and dragged me away to go grab a coffee. I was hysterical……my baby was hurt, and I didn't want to leave.

We returned to emergency to find my son in a cast. He was awake, and it looked like he was licking a popsicle. On closer inspection, he wasn't actually licking the treat……he was stoned and watching Harry Potter! We took him home and all was good. Throughout the time he was in a cast, he never complained and handled it far better than I could. His principal said it best: "Kids get hurt but are incredibly resilient little people."

Kids can be expensive. I'm not talking the costs to raise a child. I'm talking about the "accidental costs." Example: when the big flat screen craze hit, I was in with both feet. It was time to replace my old Panasonic Gaoo tv with a 50" new Panasonic

LCD. I was pumped and didn't care about the $1500 price tag. I wanted that tv. I taught my kids to be careful around dad's new pride and joy.

One morning, I went downstairs, turned on the tv to watch SportsCentre and discovered that there was a cracked, spider effect at the corner of the screen. I didn't know what was going on and went upstairs and mentioned it to my wife. She replied, "better talk to your son." Phillip was about 8 years old and I walked into his bedroom and before I could say anything, he became upset. Now, you need to know, and Phillip will now know, I'm a sucker when my kids get upset. Phillip's lip curls and you can see genuine sadness in his face. How could I be upset with this precious little boy. Still, I put on a stern face, trying to not to cry because my boy was sad, and asked what happened. Apparently, while riding the exercise bike, the remote control got stuck in the handle. Phillip turned the bike over to dislodge the control and accidentally hit the tv.

In my best stern voice, I told Phillip he would be coming with me as I bought a new tv so that he could see what these things cost. Off to Best Buy. I ended up with a brand new 55" Panasonic, complete with surround sound system and DVD player and paid far less than I had prior. I got a better system! A new toy-woohoo! But, I had to try and teach my son a lesson. But, it was too damn hard. Yes, Phillip learned a tough lesson, but daddy got new stuff!

During the ensuing years, my kids joined various sports team and I usually volunteered in some capacity or another. My daughter decided baseball would be her game. Early in her sporting life, she was placed at third base, the hot corner. I was a little concerned, as parents are, that she was playing a dangerous position. Sure enough, a hot shot was hit directly at her. Sarah calmly snagged the ball and made the throw to first in true professional form. I sat there for a moment, my jaw having dropped in surprise, then there was the "yep, that's my daughter" moment. Sarah not only had an arm, but holy hell could she hit. Many championship games were won after a homer or a grand slam. It was such a pleasure to occasionally coach or ump games.

My son played hockey and soccer and was amazing at both. In his first year of hockey, the kid scored 41 goals. Tip to parents: skip skating lessons and go right to hockey. Trust me, they learn to skate quite quickly. Saturdays became my favourite day of the week: hockey day. Watching my boy on the ice, playing very well, supporting my team and being an all-round nice guy makes me smile to this day.

Both of my kids received "Spirit Awards" when they graduated grade school. Each Catholic school awards this award to the student who not only embodies Catholic values but are great local citizens. A ceremony is held at the Board office and it's a pretty big deal. Another example that as parents, we did something right.

Yes, there are trials and tribulations when you raise a family. Now, my kids are grown up and are in the midst of post secondary educational pursuits. Both Sarah and Phillip were honours students in high school and there is no reason to believe they won't maintain this type of academic pursuit as they move forward.

As dads, we tend to do things we don't want to do, but, for the sake of the kids, we do it. A good example of this was a trip to Canada's Wonderland. You have to understand something about my son: he has zero fear. Phillip convinced the old man to ride The Behemoth, at the time, Canada's steepest and fastest roller coaster. I looked at my wife and there was no way she was going to ride it. Summoning all the courage I could muster, I relented. As the line inched closer to the ride, my heart was pounding. My son, dumbass that he was, was too excited.

Its now your turn. You get on the ride and, unlike other older coasters, you sit on a seat, similar in design to an oversized bicycle seat and a cheap, hard plastic restraint is placed over your thighs......that's it. I'm tall, but my feet wouldn't touch the floor. As we ascend up into the sky and climb to a height of oh, about 25,000 feet, you can imagine that this is the moment in time you'll finally have a heart attack. You then reach the summit and start to plummet at 750 miles per hour to your death. I swear to god, I was hanging on to the bottom of my seat so tightly, my survival depended on me not letting go. As we're hurtling down, I saw highway 400 in the distance and was absolutely sure my seat would detach at this point and I'd be thrust at Mach 1 to the highway where I would be run over by a Tim Hortons delivery truck. I look over at my son and he's laughing his ass off-little jerk.

I'm not about to enter the afterlife and the ride does get better. As we come to a stop at the end of the ride, my legs are like two pieces of pasta and I can barely walk. My little jerk son looks at me, smiles and says, "let's go again Dad." I grounded him for six weeks after that.

Video games were always a riot in our house. I was the master of Guitar Hero, or so I thought. No one could play "For Those About to Rock" better than this guy. That was until I realized I was on the easy level and Phillip showed that he could kick my ass quite easily. NHL games were especially brutal. Little putz used to beat me up all the time as I didn't know how to use the controls. Give me an old Atari any day.

As a dad, I will admit I made some bad parenting decisions along the way. You need to take training and pass a couple of tests in order to drive, yet there is zero formal training to become a parent. You learn as you go. At the end of the day, my children have grown into incredible people and as parents, we had a lot to do with that. However, once the kids start to grow, they start to make their own decisions and learn by trial by error. As they have grown into young adults, they know that their parents are always there for them and that they can always count on us.

Parenting is incredibly rewarding. I urge new parents to be as involved in your children as you can. Mentor them, teach them life skills and model the way. I cannot express enough that I love my children with all my heart. I'm not a perfect dad, but I am a proud dad.

Alcoholics Anonymous Saves Lives

"Hi, my name is Gerry and I'm an alcoholic"

I saw something on Twitter the other day that, well, pissed me off beyond normal. A poster indicated that an alcoholic father can't be a good role model for his kids. Before I chose to deal with my addiction, I may have thought that this opinion may have merit. But in today's society, we have learned that an addiction is considered a mental illness, we're (hopefully) teaching our kids tolerance, understanding and compassion.

This post is meant to provide some insight into the road to recovery that non-alcoholics may not completely understand. Alcoholics Anonymous, is by name, anonymous. I will not disclose identities of those I have met......this defeats the purpose of AA. Some choose not to disclose their addiction. There is a stigma attached to being an alcoholic, same as there is a stigma to having a weight problem or if one suffers from depression. And there is the point: **Stigma**. We, as a population, tend to form opinions about topics we do not understand or no very little about. Want proof? I'm a living example of someone who had strong opinions about addictions and, as usual, I didn't have a clue what the hell I was talking about.

It was late December 2016 that I came to the realization that I may have a drinking problem. My drinking was way beyond control. The more I drank, the more I needed. Daily trips to the LCBO in my wheelchair became the norm. I'd be shaky, couldn't eat, was very sick, and generally speaking, life had gone to hell. I thought my problems in life were unique, that no one cared......all the usual self pity thoughts. A friend recognized, via my unusual social media posts, that there was something wrong. The friend showed up one day and, after some discussion, convinced me to come to an AA meeting. Upon arrival, I wheeled in, unshaven, looking sick as can be and feeling very ashamed. AA was, in my mind, a place for, how do I put this, a bunch of people who lacked the personal strength to control themselves. Yet, here I was.

Having never been to a meeting, I didn't know what to expect, so I kept quiet. There were about a dozen people there and, as they started to share, I was in tears. I couldn't believe I was this weak and pathetic. Then something in my head and I did something I don't usually do: I listened. I started hearing other as they spoke and shared their stories and I realized that my issues were similar to others. The more I listened, the more I learned, and I started to feel slightly better. I was still detoxing, but the symptoms started to subside. I really thought that AA was preachy and too religious for me. Again, I was wrong.

I swore to myself that I would give this whole AA thing a go. I stopped buying booze, started to eat again, attended meetings and, most importantly, I started to "work the program". This is the critical piece to success, and its very obvious to state, but you get what you put into it. I was given a copy of The Big Book and took this very seriously. The first step, **accepting that you're powerless over alcohol** is key. Reminding yourself everyday that you have now lost the privilege to drink and that each day you don't drink is a victory. I was taught that there are many ways to assist with your daily battle: attend meetings, meditate, yoga (tried it.... not for me!), writing a journal and so on. I turned to starting my book.

I met so many people at AA. People of all ages, men and women, moms and dads, from every occupation. Nurses, chefs, teachers, labourers and more. Some, like me, were new to the program while others had been sober for years and years. Some, while drunk, found themselves in trouble at home, work, or in a couple of cases, with the law. Many experienced a wake-up call, and, because they reached out for help, started to attend meetings. Some folks were in so much pain and were experiencing so much guilt. Some were celebrating sobriety and painting for a us a picture of what a good sober life looks like.

I'd continue to attend meetings. My family and a very good friend would pick me up in my wheelchair and take me to and from meetings. Physically, I was starting to feel amazing. From a mental point of view, a little better. In AA, they refer to giving yourself over a "higher power". Many think this means turning yourself over to God. What it actually means is that if you turn to a higher power, like a sponsor, a friend, your partner, a cup of coffee or a pencil, it doesn't matter. Its about turning to someone or something that gives you the inspiration, support or n ear to listen that aids you in your drive for sobriety.

I worked the steps. A self inventory was needed. Taking a good look into yourself is not the most enjoyable exercise, but critical. The next step requires one to admit to the things we have done wrong, examining our poor behaviour. This is a turning point for some. Either you admit to your past mistakes and accept responsibility, or it can actually drive you back to the bottle. No one wants to beat themselves down like this. But, in order to change your behaviour, you need to understand what qualities about yourself that need to be changed. For me, I realized I was a selfish, ignorant bastard. I was having flashbacks of the crappy things I had done. During my various binges, I'd be so wasted, that days would go by and I'd ignore my phone. One time, my son was concerned and ended up calling the police who came to check on me. I had had the heart attack in November, so he was really concerned. I remember one of the cops, as he was leaving, say to me **"don't be an asshole, call your son."** Not the best role model for my boy. This was tough to acknowledge. So, I swore to stay sober, not just for me, but for the people I loved and that loved me.

In February 2017, I was admitted to Parkwood Hospital to start the rehab process to get fitted for my first prosthetic leg and to learn to walk again. I was in a wheelchair for 8 months, so I was a tad rusty. I was still sober and the stay in the hospital made it easier to remain booze free. I was walking again!!! What a feeling. I was gaining some weight and was not free from that freaking wheelchair. I got home after my stay, walked like a madman and life was getting good. Then I made the mistake.... I mean **THE MISTAKE**. I told myself, during a trip to Barrie with a friend, that I could handle a drink or two.

I started drinking again, in my mind socially, so it would be okay...right? I returned from this trip and went back to AA and admitted I was back to day one. I was embraced and accepted. Many had been through the same thing as me. I continued with the program and stayed sober.... until I slipped again in March 2017. Now I was really hitting the bottle hard. I was back to work, the person I loved was back in my world, so what the hell was going on? I never showed up at AA drunk, but acted like all was good. I kept feeling sorry for myself.... lost a leg, heart attack, divorced, crappy job. Everything came to a head April 17th when in a drunken stupor, I killed myself.

I'm not going to re-hash this incident. It was during my time in the hospital that it hit me like a ton of bricks. I was carrying a hell of a lot of baggage that I hadn't dealt with. While attending a professionally led Addictions Group at the hospital, I learned about triggers, coping skills and how to forgive myself. But there was one step I was not looking forward to: AA Steps 8 & 9, developing a list of all those individuals I hurt and to make amends. This step would take some time.

After a month long stay in hospital, I went back to AA and again, was hugged and never ever judged for falling down. Those attending the meetings reminded me that its a tough process, but there is hope. One of my biggest supporters has been sober for 27 years!!!During one incident, while in hospital October 2017 to have part of my left foot removed, a member saw me at the hospital, hugged me and reminded me to stay strong. (Being diabetic, alcohol is a big no no. Drinking so much certainly didn't help. This was so inspiring. I'd see another AA member in the public and see a walking example of how great sobriety can be.

I did a lot of damage to not only others, especially the ones I love and respect and value so much. I also did a ton of damage to myself, physically and mentally. I continued, and still do, to attend meetings. I learned to manage my stress, accepted what I had done, still carried a bit of guilt. but decided life was way better being.... you know.... alive. Shortly after my one-year anniversary, I was having flashbacks. I spoke to someone who I respect greatly, and he reminded me that you have to keep working the program. I was dreading steps 8 and 9, but it had to be done.

I began what I call "The Apology Tour". I recapped my lousy behaviour and asked for forgiveness. Most forgave me.... some did not. **My family forgave me.** I had lost a couple of great friends and while I will forever be sorry for what I had done to them, I needed to accept the fact that I damaged them too much and they decided to carry on life without me in it. The toughest was apologizing to my son. This incredible person stuck by his drunken old man, supporting me when he could, picking me up and dusting me off when I needed it and occasionally kicked my butt when I needed it. He saw his father at his worst. But he hung in there...checking in with me and visiting me in the hospital. As a parent, I must have taught him something right. To this day, he continues to tell me everyday that he is proud of me and loves me. I am so damn lucky and so incredibly proud of him......more than you can imagine.

I hurt someone else that is so important in my life: my greatest cheerleader and friend. Everyday she tells me how she is so proud of what I've done with my life and is excited for the great future ahead of me. And she forgave me when I didn't deserve it. She saved my life, literally, and has stood by my side each and everyday.

I am alive today for many reasons. One of them are the great people at AA. The volunteers who chair the meetings, the people who attend these meetings who continue to share and inspire me are to be admired and thanked. Yes, I highly recommend getting professional counselling to deal with the baggage that has led us to drink. But Alcoholics Anonymous is always there, accepting you with open arms and with no fear of being judged. There are dozens of meetings every week here in London, as there are in most cities. Get to a meeting......you won't be sorry. Yes, it will hurt a bit and like any struggle, it can be challenging and difficult.

I am not bragging when I say this: I have been sober for a year and a half. I recently published my first book with two more on the way. I am now healthy, happy and productive again. Most importantly, for me, I was not abandoned by those in my life that I adore and love. To those people.... thank you is all I can say. I will continue to prove that your faith in me was worth your time, support and hard work. What I am saying is that there is **HOPE**....you just have to work at it. Trust me, it worth it!
To those who I have hurt: I am so sorry. You didn't deserve this. You're great people and deserved better from me. I will do better...I promise.

To the non-alcoholic: Learn a little bit about addiction. and maybe exercise some patience, understanding and care. Knowing what I know now, I am embarrassed to have had such negative views and opinions that I did. Removing stigma requires all of us to educate ourselves on the subject, show compassion and be supportive. Remember: **#sicknotweak**
If you are struggling, don't know where to turn, find an AA meeting. Check out their websites...some great stuff to be found. If you're afraid, you can find me on Facebook (gerrylahay) or Twitter (@GerryLaHay). Send me a message.... I'm here to help. Many did it for me....

Getting Out of the Byron Bubble

In my very first column, I wrote about living in Byron in good ole London Ontario, a very busy life and how I was oblivious to and ready didn't care as to what was happening in the rest of the city. I am not picking on anyone from Byron or any other suburb. I am speaking from my own experience.

I knew we had homelessness, drugs on the street, a dying downtown and I really didn't pay much attention to it. I was in my comfy ranch home in Byron with my big backyard and two cars in the driveway. I didn't give much thought to issues those with disabilities faced or crime, unless it was in my neighbourhood. Oh, we had crime in West London, but, unless it affected me, I didn't give it much thought. This wasn't a conscious decision to ignore it. Life was moving pretty damn quick with work and family. I had a pre-conceived notion, not a nice one, about what the Wortley Village was like, nor would I even consider going to The Wortley to eat. Downtown was dead to me...dirty, vacant store fronts with not much to do, so I avoided it like the plague unless I was off to see a Knight's game or a concert. I hadn't been in any downtown shops in over 25 years. On my drive to work, I'd pass The Salvation Army and The Men's Mission without giving any thought to what was happening inside their walls. Woodfield? Never heard of it.

I know the city fairly well thanks to my old days at Domino's Pizza. Or, at least I thought I did. Geographically I knew the city, but not the neighbourhoods or the people. I'd take the kids to various sports fields and arenas, but really didn't pay any attention to my surroundings. I ate at chain restaurants in Westmount, shopped at Masonville and the Superstore on

Oxford W. Don't get me wrong, great places to shop and dine. I drove everywhere, never taking the LTC.

I used social media like Facebook and Twitter differently than I use it now, therefore I was almost blind to what was really happening out there. I was involved in politics minimally, only caring when it affected me and my family. Yeah, I read the Free Press and watched the local news and was up to date on current affairs. The realization that I was living life with such tunnel vision dawned on me in September 2015 when I left my marriage and I moved to Old South.

This is when I discovered and came to absolutely love the Wortley Village. The Old South Pub, Valu Mart, Fire Roasted, The Black Walnut and Home Hardware quickly became my favourites. Valu Mart took some getting used to as I found their prices a little higher, but the staff!!! Wow. I was, and still am to some degree, a Tims guy simply because of the number of locations, but give me a Fire Roasted or a Black Walnut any day! I was introduced to Mai's Café and Bistro where I found the greatest damn Cashew Chicken and Pad Thai in the city!!!

Then there is The Wortley. Ahhhh.... The Wortley. Nothing makes me happier than the $4.99 Wortley breakfast (served before 3:00 p.m.). The staff are exceptional, always greeting us so warmly and always knowing what we want. Great neighbourhood bar and grill.

There is a sense of community as I walk around The Village. Homes that are nicely maintained, lots of friendly people walking their dogs and there seems to be something always going on. In my 18 years in Byron, even though it is a beautiful neighbourhood, I never got the sense of community except on

Canada Day. Byron has great eateries like the Freehouse, Bernies and one of my favourite Chinese food restaurants, Chinatown. The Byron Mini Mart is run by an incredibly friendly group of Korean women, and whenever I'm in Byron, I try and find an excuse to buy something. But the neighbourhood lacks something.....

Living in Old South had an impact on how I travelled. I could now walk downtown and park the car more often. I discovered many little things along my walk. Carfrae Park, when not over run with a few "campers" is actually quite peaceful. At the corner of Carfrae and Carfrae (yes.... that is what the street signs say), there is a little convenience store that sits on the original Supertest gas stations. As you cross the path on Richmond, you'll stumble across a nice little park at the end of South St, home to, if my memory serves me correctly, you'll find that this was the site of an old soap factory that closed in the early 1900s. Other than dropping my daughter off for work at Thames Park, I had never explored the beauty of the park and how peaceful this little gem was......especially in the heart of the city.

During my walks that led me down town, I'd pass the Salvation Army and was a little alarmed at the number of people hanging around outside. If I was walking along Horton, I'd stop into Edgar & Joes for a quick coffee. I rediscovered City Lights Bookstore and found Grooves on Dundas St. I enjoy my writing time at Coffee Culture, especially when they have their warm pistachio muffins for sale. I looked at amazement at the architecture of the downtown buildings, stunned at how old they were, yet they managed to stand the test of time in an ever-evolving London.

I came to enjoy Windsor Ave and Baker St. Who wouldn't love such a charming neighbourhood? When I was fitted with a prosthetic leg, I really embraced the opportunity to walk (sometimes you don't appreciate the simple things until its gone.). I was walking everywhere. I fell in love with The Church Key, Victoria Park and St. Peter's Basilica. When I moved from The Village up to Oxford and Maitland, I explored Old North. Pall Mall, Piccadilly, Maitland and Hellmuth....what a spectacular area of the city. I found Piccadilly Park, and if memory serves me correctly, the site of the original Western Fair. I'd walk downtown and witnessed the beauty of Woodfield along the way. I never really appreciated Victoria Park until the last couple of years....an empty Victoria Park when not used for the various festivals it hosts each summer.

But I also discovered a few things I sort of knew existed but was blind to......street people and drugs. Something you don't see a lot of in Byron. I bring this up because it would be completely irresponsible of me to only think that we have such a beautiful city and turn a blind eye to the harsh realities I've come to see. Our city has major problems....and they only seem to be getting worse.

During my time in a wheelchair, I was using the LTC a lot more so there were transfer times to sit and wait, so I'd pickup prescriptions at Rexall (sad to see this location closed.... wonderful staff) or grab a coffee and people watch. I was immediately stunned when I saw the number of street people. And the presence of street preachers. And the drugs. And the serious mental issues many of these folks were suffering. Now, with a new perspective on the world thanks to my......you know.... that little drinking problem I had, I saw this environment in a totally different way.

During my various trips downtown, I witnessed violence, sadness and hopelessness. I watched on too many occasions, drug deals, whether on the street, in parking lots and alleys and in the Tims parking lot on York street. I've maneuvered around people sleeping on the street, sometimes taking up a whole sidewalk. One day, a group had set up a little tarp tent in front of the old GT's and I witnessed the police and the City remove it. The group of people would then retreat to behind the building and then return later and set up again. I would see people sleeping under the overhang at the Spriet Building at Richmond and York. Despite the efforts of the City, I'd see countless used needles and garbage everywhere.

Even today, when I stopped by the Salvation Army to drop something off for a friend, I see people lined up to use their food bank. Dozens of people hanging around the front of the building or at the Tim Hortons on Horton St. I now live on Oxford St E and on a daily basis, I see street people walking up and down the street, some pushing grocery carts containing what belongings they have left in this world. There is one particular gentleman I see regularly who walks down the street, no shoelaces and quite often, he'll just walk out into the middle of traffic, either not paying attention, not aware or simply, in the hopes of getting hit? One day, I found a young woman sleeping under a sleeping bag under a tree on the property I rent. I approached her to make sure she was okay, and it was very apparent that either there was a mental health issue, or she was under the influence of something. A hospital band could be seen on her wrist. Not knowing about London Cares, I called police to make sure she was okay. Officers arrived and took her to a safe place.

I know we have a serious drug problem in this city and I'm very aware that there just aren't enough mental health services available. I completely get that we have a severe lack of affordable housing. I was on the list at one point and was advised it could take five years or more. At the time, I was in a wheelchair, abusing alcohol and was forced to live in an apartment that was no where near accessible. I came very close to being homeless. I was lucky, and I was saved by a friend......something that not many can say.

I am incredibly frustrated.... I know very little on how to solve this problem...I just don't have the answers. I see steps are being taken to address these issues. The Middlesex London Health Unit has opened a Temporary Overdose Prevention that is showing a high number of users and lives have been saved. The process to open a permanent site is well underway. The City of London is working on solutions that will address the drug problem, homelessness and poverty. This process will take time......and money. With our city approaching a municipal election, we need to ensure that the candidates that win make these issues a high priority. Our province has let us down and we must be unrelenting on lobbying our politicians to focus on these critical issues. We need to provide enhanced and accessible drug and alcohol treatment, vastly improved mental health services and housing.

The purpose of this post was not to depress people. We have a beautiful and vibrant city......we really do. Get out and explore! But there is a dark side that many of us either ignore or don't know enough about. We can't continue to live in a bubble and turn a blind eye to what is happening around us. Let's promise to listen, learn, sympathize, understand and together, find solutions. I thank the many advocates and organizations that continue to support our most vulnerable. You are truly amazing.

Health Care and London Hospitals

Recently, a video with Jim Carrey made the rounds of social media and I had to chuckle for a moment. His claim that our health care is amazing and free is only partly true. Our health care is truly amazing, although overburdened, in my experience, but it is costly. Since June 2016, I have spent significant time in hospital. Here are the moments I have experienced and examples of how the health care system does cost money.

Much of what you'll read below will not surprise many of you. Before I begin, during my previous married life, I paid **$900** in OHIP annually as did my spouse. We paid the highest amount due to our earnings. In addition, tens of thousands were paid in income tax, property tax and HST. My wife paid high health coverage premiums each month to ensure coverage for our family. My son's braces cost $6000. My wife's benefits only covered half. Out of pocket: **$3000**

June 2016: With a badly infected foot that became so dangerous, I lost a ton of weight and in the end, had to be rushed to the hospital. Within moments of being seen in emergency, I was informed that the foot would be amputated. The doctors and, nurses and support staff were so sincere in their sympathy, but the surgery was critical. I was very sick and in danger of dying. Within three days, I lost my foot. The surgeon was caring, and the nursing staff were incredible. I was visited by counselors, social workers and therapists, although all carried heavy caseloads and my time with them was limited. I was sent home three days later with a new pair of crutches: **Cost: $50.00.** Not having benefits, this was out of pocket and, thanks to my stupidity for not dealing with this sooner, I was also out of a paycheque for a few weeks. I had to scramble to find equipment such as a wheelchair, shower bench, walker and so on. Luckily, I discovered the Consistatory Club.

November 1st, 2016: I suffered a major heart attack. London EMS and the team at University Hospital saved my life. I can't say enough about the speed and quality of care. At discharge, I was given several prescriptions that I never filled as I could not afford them. **EMS Bill: $50.00**

November 6th, 2016: Two more minor heart attacks. Reason: Couldn't afford the drugs. The hospital covered the first round, but I would be on the hook after that. I went on Ontario Works temporarily after my employer laid me off. This covered the drugs for awhile.

There were times I could not afford the drugs I needed. And I was suffering from major depression and anxiety with, seemingly, nowhere to turn. It was late January 2017, laid off work, OW coverage not helping ends meet. Thanks to the generosity of many people, I survived. I was then notified that I was to be admitted to Parkwood Hospital for a month to begin the process of being fitted for a prosthetic leg. The initial cost would be approximately **$12,000.... yes.... $12,000!!** The Assistive Devices Program covers 70% (**$8400**) while a **$1000** grant from War Amps would be expected. That left me with an anticipated out of pocket bill of approximately **$2,600**. I panicked but was told to not worry about that and to proceed with the rehab at Parkwood.

I cannot say enough about the bloody incredible team at Parkwood during this stay. The fantastic professionals spent an extraordinary time re-teaching me to walk and to live again.

There are so many programs that you take part in: rehab, physio, occupational and recreational. I spent time with a therapist where I played on a Wii. This helped with balance and coordination, something we take for granted. I spent time in a kitchen, outdoors and constant re-fittings for my leg. Great patience and care is taken to ensure that when you are discharged, you're set for success. After leaving hospital, there are regular follow up appointments. During my stay, I was contacted by War Amps in Ottawa. It seems the prosthetic company, London Prosthetics had submitted a request to have Wars Amps cover the **$2600** I was to pay. After a conference call and interview, Wars Amps graciously covered the rest of my bill!

Now walking, I was optimistic about life again.... for a little while. March 2017, I returned to work and lost drug coverage. I have Type 2 Diabetes. Insulin, needles and other supplies cost money. A box of insulin is $100.00 alone. The needles are $30/box. Add in the heart drugs and anti-anxiety pills, I was up to approx. **$400.00**/month, all out of my pocket, which was money I did not have. A trip to the dentist was out of the question.

With diabetes, my eyesight continues to slowly deteriorate. A basic exam is covered through OHIP, but the 65,000-layer eye scan that is used to see the progression of the eye damage cost me **$95.00**, again, out of pocket. A prescription for glasses was issued as I needed stronger glasses. **$300-400** would cover the cost. So, I skipped the glasses, instead wearing the older broken ones I already had.

April 2017: Returning to work, off anti-depression meds and battling alcoholism, I attempted a nearly successful suicide. I've written about this before so no need to speak about it again. The main point being that I found that this thirty day stay at LHSC was both positive and negative. I'm mentally healthy today thanks to many factors, but it became very apparent we do not have enough resources and access to mental health care.

September 2017: remaining foot becomes infected. (Long story about an infection that won't leave my body). Due to mistreatment by a doctor at the Cellulitis Clinic at St. Joes, infection spreads like wildfire. A plastic surgeon is called in and it's decided to amputate. Seeing I've already lost a leg, the surgeon admits me and amputates two toes during two separate surgeries. The care I receive at University Hospital was exceptional. I need to wear a special shoe upon discharge after a two week stay. Cost: **$45.00**

My family doctor encouraged me to apply for ODSP due to the amputations and supports my application. I am approved within three weeks. ODSP advises that I should go on permanent Canada disability. Woohoo....drug coverage. I would eventually apply for and am approved for disability. Between ODSP and Disability, I'm covered although the monthly support equals about $6.85/hr. Not quite enough to live on, but I manage. Disability allows for a bit more freedom on earning extra income, so I write a novel. This was a dream come true and while I haven't sold a ton of copies, I'm productive and able to make a couple extra bucks.

Late December 2017: infection in foot worsens. I'm quickly admitted to hospital at St. Joes where half of my foot is removed. Again, care is terrific. I'm again sized for a special show: another **$45.00**. I'm then sent to Parkwood while I recover, under heavy drug IV's and a vacuum attached to the remaining stump. I'm now in the Complex Care ward at

Parkwood and the care was, to be polite, absolutely terrible. I leave hospital, now under the wonderful care of VON at the Florence St clinic. I'm provided with supplies and after a few weeks, the vacuum is removed, and I'm discharged from their care.

As of this writing, a year after the initial surgery was performed, I'm still recovering. The wound is still open (although almost closed). Trips to the HULC Clinic every couple of weeks and the on-going infection make recovery a little challenging. I buy supplies such as gauze, cling and others, out of pocket. A ten pack of gauze pads cost **$10.00.** I've bought a lot of supplies this past year, along with a continuing supply of socks and shoes that become contaminated over time with the infection.

Last week, I finally ordered new glasses.... this old guy's eyes are slowly losing focus. Glasses have gone up in price!!! With ODSP coverage, I paid **$100.00** out of pocket.

Bottom line is this: I have had, for the most part, fantastic health care, especially over the past two years. Yes, I am fortunate to have coverage now and our health care is far superior and cheaper than many countries around the world. I think of the many workers out in our community, struggling to make ends meet and seeing their own health care deteriorate since they cannot afford the cost. So, for those who claim health care is free, I strongly disagree.

Many face long wait times in emergency or wait months or even years for referral appointments and surgeries. Mental health patients are laying on stretchers behind curtains for days waiting to me admitted and managed. The Ford government claims to take health care seriously yet cuts the promised funds for mental health. Hospitals are required to balance budgets and end up cutting services and staff. With an aging population, a drug and homelessness crisis very prevalent, and mental health illnesses growing, something has to give. Our governments need to step up and solve our health care problems.... **NOW.** If we don't see immediate improvements, this situation will only get worse......and that scares the hell out of me.

Social Media: What the Hell is Going On?

With the 2018 Municipal Election behind us, this may be a good time to re-focus ourselves.

> For every action, there is an equal and opposite reaction, plus a social media overreaction.

Before I even begin, I have to remember I've been guilty of unacceptable behaviour in the past. Over the last few years, I've toned down my behaviour and try, most days to be respectful. A pal on Twitter (a Pantsless Club member) reminds me once in awhile that we can participate and disagree but need to keep it respectful.

I've been online for almost two decades now. Back to the days of ICQ, MSN Chat and chat rooms were the popular means of social media back in the day. And yes, there was bullying and harassment back then as well.

Today, I enjoy Facebook and Twitter for a variety of reasons: entertainment, engagement, politics and to stay informed. My goal some days is to entertain, maybe make someone smile or laugh, hopefully some posts cause some to stop and think and if I can, help those in need. (Yes....occasionally.... some self promotion. I have no shame!). What I am seeing the past few months is, to put it mildly, very disappointing.

Several things I've learned during my 20 years on social media. First and foremost is the unacceptable amount of bullying I see. A couple of examples come to mind. There is a guy I follow who has admitted to poor "assholey" behaviour in the past. From what I'm seeing, he is making a concerted effort to make changes to the way he is perceived. His conduct is, for the most part, respectful, insightful and he adds value to my Twitter experience. Lately, I'm seeing quite a few folks trashing and bashing him, not directly, but consistently. A couple of these people I used to have a great deal respect for are jumping on and this respect is dwindling quickly. Why are we seeing this type of piling on? What are we, a bunch of kids who don't know any better? Who among us haven't conducted ourselves in a manner that is unacceptable? I know I have, and I'm committed to not acting like this again. Why can't we recognize that this person has been contrite, should be forgiven and given an opportunity to prove that he is changing his way? I think we should. My behaviour in the past not only on social media, but out in the world was horrific at times. If I didn't make changes, sustain proper adult and respectful behaviour, I'd never be forgiven and would be spending my life alone. People gave me a chance to make changes, we should allow others to do the same.

I see so many people and organizations trying with all their might to do great things for this city. I cannot express my appreciation for what these outstanding Londoners do for our city enough. True heroes in my world. Yet, I see some who do nothing but insult, denigrate and criticize these efforts. What is especially appalling is the fact that the naysayers have done absolutely nothing to help solve the problems we face. Talk is cheap.... get off the damn computer and help make the changes you want to see in this world. You can sit and quote web sources and argue all you want. But unless you help guide change, you have very little credibility.

I pride myself with the fact that I have and will continue to stand up to bullying. I have taught my kids to do the same. Some suggest block or mute. I simply will not do this. People need to be called on their behaviour. The golden rule needs to be applied here. I'm quite sure that those doling out the abuse would be quite upset if the tables were turned on them. I've been called many things, including recently someone referred to me as a snowflake. Me....a snowflake? Those who know me will laugh out loud at hearing this. I will simply not stand silently, and watch people get torn down.

I have, for the past couple of years, tried to be more respectful. I will disagree with people but try to stick to facts and not make it personal. In years past, I would argue sometimes just for the sake of arguing. You'd say the sky was blue and I'd argue it was purple and call you an idiot in the process. That has changed. I value other's opinions and respect their courage to speak. Sometimes, listening is learning. However, lately I see some trying to force their opinions on others by posting post threads and at times, they seem to be almost yelling. Spirited debate is terrific, but we need to tone down the disrespectful behaviour and allow others to hold their own values and opinions.

The anonymous posters are the worst. I call them "drive by shooters". They lack the courage to put a name and a face to a post. They jump in, post some of the most ignorant things this salty old guy has seen in my 52 years of my existence. I have zero tolerance for these gutless and cowardly people. As another one of my favourite people (ice cream aficionado) on Twitter would say: "delete your account."

I learned a lesson about a year ago from a Londoner who I admire and respect immensely (she knows who she is.... hint: pumpkin spice and all sorts licorice lover). Stop, wait and don't be so quick to judge. Wait for the facts to come out before spouting off with an uninformed opinion. I jumped all over someone without taking time to pause. In the end, I was wrong and quite frankly, I was very embarrassed at my behaviour. Yesterday, I saw something that was happening to a local candidate. I was about to jump in with both feet and lose it. I waited and later found that the candidate actually handled this incident with class and care.

Quick question: when did we earn the right to call people/politicians ignorant names in public like this? Hey, I disagree with politicians and people all the time, but refrain from the name calling. I suspect a great many behave differently hiding behind a computer or smartphone and sure as heck wouldn't act like that face to face. Listen, I used to swear so badly, I'd embarrass a sailor (no offense sailors.... figure of speech), but there have been times I have sat with a dropped jaw after reading some of the things I see.

But, having said all of this, what has really caught me off guard, are the attacks and threats levelled at women who step up and help guide our worlds. To hear and see racist comments, insults and (holy crap) death threats has really stunned me. I've been at a loss for words. Seems the gutless people who make these comments think a woman is an easier target because I certainly don't hear of many men facing this type of disturbing behaviour. This criminal activity, and this shouldn't have to be said, is completely unacceptable and needs to stop. I know some have reported this behaviour to police and I encourage those who haven't to do so immediately. I am so sorry that you have to face this and can't tell you enough how encouraged and grateful to you for standing strong.

Years ago, while working at Western, I was the target of a stalker. The person was making comments and threats against me and my family. This person described my car, my home and made comments about what he would do to my wife. I was concerned but didn't really give it much credence. As a manager, I know that at times, former employees leave with a negative attitude and threaten all the time. Quick story: when I started at Domino's, the store I was to start at was set on fire by a former employee.... FIVE years after being fired. With this in mind, I paid attention, but at the same time, blew it off and told nobody. Eventually, I brought it to my wife who strongly encouraged me to call police. Again, while a little concerned, I didn't act. I was using an Executive Coach at the time, trying to hone my management skills. I mentioned it to him in passing and he was quite alarmed. I showed him the screenshots and he was very alarmed.

I went back to work, carrying on my business. As I was leaving one building, I saw my coach leaving the campus police office.

He had reported this behaviour o police who took it far more seriously than I did. London Police were brought in and an investigation was launched. They ran into a roadblock with Yahoo who refused to cooperate, and the investigation ended. However, for the next few months, I was always looking behind me. Now, imagine the terror and fear my family went through. And now, imagine the fear that these brave female politicians must be enduring when all they are doing is working so hard for our community. Think about your cowardly actions before acting.

The types of behaviour I have written about are the exacts things we teach our kids NOT to do. We teach them to treat others with respect, refrain from bullying and insulting others, yet we're not modelling the way for the younger generation. We're quick to consequence our kids yet we turn around and refer to someone on social media as an asshole. Seems kind of hypocritical doesn't it? My son follows me on social media and its my responsibility to show him the way, although he's a pretty respectful person all on his own. But, take a moment to think about this....

I know I sound like a preachy old guy. I have a very tough skin most days. Since I've become disabled, I have faced discrimination, ignorant comments and a couple of times, the threat of violence. Some days, I can take it.... I consider the source. But other days, these actions can and do hurt. I implore you: please think about your social media before you post. Can we get back to some sort of civility? Let's continue some debate, let's even disagree. Let's bring back some wisdom, humour, information and do some good in this world.

A tip of the cap to those who keep it respectful, informative and enjoyable. There are far more terrific "Twitterers" (is this a word.... well it is now) to follow than there are bullies. So, as a dad, I end with this: "Play nicely kids!"

An Employer of Choice!

> " Employees who believe that management is concerned about them as a whole person - not just an employee - are more productive, more satisfied, more fulfilled. Satisfied employees mean satisfied customers, which leads to profitability." Anne M. Mulcahy

RENEE, I'M THE BOSS AROUND HERE ... AND DON'T YOU EVER FORGET IT!

With the recent goings-on at Queens Park by Doug Ford and his attack on lower income workers, I found myself asking if employers are doing enough to motivate, retain and reward their staff. There is an expectation amongst some that government is responsible for creating laws and bills that direct businesses on how much to pay staff, health and safety laws etc. This leads me to ask businesses: what is your company doing to ensure that your staff are paid enough to ensure a decent standard of living.

I speak with a lot of folks who are the workers in a business and I'm still astounded at the conditions they work in. I would have thought in 2018, we'd see better leadership and working conditions. From what I'm hearing and seeing, I'm wrong.... again. I was in a leadership role of some sorts since, well, forever. In my many years in the Food and Beverage business, I worked for/with three major companies: Domino's, Western and Compass Group. Each company spent an extraordinary amount of time educating its leaders. This ensured not only profitability but most importantly, how to lead a motivated team. Some of the training and education I took during my time:

"Don't Be A Jerk Boss"

Certificate in Management: Harvard Manage Mentor

Active Listening

Mental First Aid

Disc Personality Training (how to work with different personalities)

Health & Safety Certification: Levels One and Two

Management and Performance

Performance Management and Progressive Discipline

Food Safety Certification

Human Resources

And much, much more. Each and every one of these programs, even if it was financially themed, focused on the benefits of a motivated employee. Whether it was profit and loss analysis, health and safety or first aid, the main point was that as a business or a leader, the team we worked with needed to be the number one focus. Read this the other day: as a leader, have you heard this about yourself?

Is a micro-manager
Is not trustworthy or doesn't keep promises
Gave a poor rating on the employee's performance review
Gave no raise, or not enough of a raise
Does not stand behind decisions made by employees
Is moody
Is a "know it all" and does not listen
Has questionable ethics
Is disrespectful

https://peterstark.com

Now take a look at your business and ask yourself:

Are my staff motivated?

Is our sick time above peer average?

Do you have high turnover?

Are you meeting revenue targets?

How are your cost controls?

Is your health and safety program working?

Are you spending too much time managing team members who are not meeting expectations and spending very little time focusing on the staff who are exceeding expectations?

Are you rewarding your team for work well done?

If any of this sounds familiar, its time to take a moment of pause and re-think your strategies. If your business is not succeeding as you have envisioned, the fault probably lies with you as the leader.

I was chatting with a friend the other day who expressed disappointment at work. It seems the kitchen team was directed to come up with weekly food specials to create some buzz. The team went ahead and came up with some incredible ideas. Problem was, management told them to complete this exercise yet there wasn't any support from the front of the house, zero marketing or social media support. The exercise failed. Now imagine the disappointment of the staff who worked hard to develop this program only to see it fail?

Another friend passed along this story: She saw a posting for a promotion. Her credentials were such that she was very qualified for the role. Approaching her manager to express an interest, the manager told her he liked her where she was, and she was too valuable to lose. So, no opportunity to grow?

This story really concerned me: a lead hand, making $14.00/hr before the minimum wage increase on January 2018. Staff are bumped up to $14 to comply with legislation. The lead hand remains at $14/hr. Now they are paid the same, but expected to not only do their job, but manage a team and be responsible for compliance of all policies and procedures?

When a team is unhappy in their work, the results can be negative:

- Increased sick time. Staff don't feel like going in to work thanks to several reasons: bad boss, uncooperative supervisors, not getting proper rest breaks
- Sales remain stagnant or actually decrease.
- Customer service complaints rise
- Turnover of staff rises. The manager is always having to recruit and train
- Workplace accidents rise as the employee loses focus
- Care isn't taken in product production

There are many ways to fix this and in turn, save great employees and watch your business grow.

> **"More than half of people who leave their jobs do so because of their relationship with their boss. Smart companies make certain their managers know how to balance being professional with being human. These are the bosses who celebrate an employee's success, empathize with those going through hard times, and challenge people, even when it hurts."**
>
> **Travis Bradberry**

Model the Way: Be the leader one can admire. Tom Monahan, founder of Domino's Pizza, believed strongly in The Golden Rule. Treat people how you want to be treated. Show your staff that you can and will work beside them as opposed to standing there with your arms crossed barking orders. Get in the trenches with them. You'll find the staff are now motivated and you've proven that you're a team!

Reward: During my time with a large company, we used to run a promotion for staff that focused on upselling and customer service. This program would run for three months. We'd set targets and, if the targets were met, those responsible would be entered into a weekly draw for a $50 gift card AND also entered into a end of promo draw for a $1000 prize, usually an iPad or whatever they chose. If I witnessed exceptional customer service, their names went into the draw. I'd conduct a customer training session, usually over a pizza dinner and we'd kick off the promo. Staff were engaged. Sales saw a double-digit increase. There was fun at work. I would spend about $2500 on this promo and it paid off. We had re-established a customer service culture that became second nature. The business, the staff and the customers benefited...a win-win for all.

Listen: Listen to your team. As the front-line staff, they have some great insight as to what is happening in the business. They're hear from the customers, their needs and wants. Take time to actively listen, meaning close your mouth and open your ears and mind. Staff who feel their boss listens feel more important to the business. Learn about your staff, their goals and desires. Nothing speaks louder than a boss who cares!

Communicate: Nothing is worse in a workplace than the lack of communication. Keep your staff up to date. Let them know about early closures if you're seasonal. Conduct informal and formal meetings, pre-shifts and emails. Set up a staff Facebook page. Staff that know as much as possible about the business will be engaged and will produce better results.

Work/life Balance: promote a healthy balance. Understand that your team has a life outside of work. Be it a teenager who plays sports or wants to attend an event or a parent who has a sick child, your team needs to know you're looking out for their needs as much as they are looking out for yours. I have a boss who had a philosophy that he really didn't care if you took time off for family or worked a short day on Fridays. He explained that I knew what my responsibilities were and the outcomes that were expected. How I got there was on me. He promoted family and leisure.

Be Honest: This is pretty straightforward. If your staff can trust you, they'll be loyal. Guaranteed.

Succession Planning: train and promote within. Give staff the opportunity to grow in your business. They'll spend less time looking for other opportunities and focus on the success of your business.

Manage! Nothing destroys morale when a manager doesn't actually manage. Companies have policies and procedures that need to be enforced. When bad employees aren't held accountable and are allowed to flaunt the rules, the good employees see this and become demotivated. Tough conversations are critical and even tougher decisions to end an employee relationship are necessary. **As Spock said in "The Wrath of Kahn": "The good of the many outweighs the good of the few or the one."** And before jumping the gun and disciplining a staff member, find out why they performed the way they did. You may be surprised.

Train: nothing sets an employee up for failure than the lack of training. Some staff train quicker than others and so be it. Take the time to not only tell staff what to do but show them how to do it and what the end result should look like. If they make a mistake, show them again. An example: I've heard and seen Chefs call their cook teams idiots or make comments like: "I thought you knew how to make that." The cook may know how to make it elsewhere but is probably unsure how you want it made.

<u>Ensure a safe work environment</u>: I cannot stress the importance of this enough. A safe work environment reduces accidents, saves you money and most importantly, protects the worker. A safe environment includes ensuring the workplace is not a toxic environment, fee from gossip, bully and harassment. I've seen several businesses lately where there is zero time spent on health and safety and this is incredibly dangerous.

Manage Yourself: Pace yourself, take time for non-work activities, focus on family. Preventing burn out will make you a much better boss.

And finally, **pay your staff a decent wage**! Don't wait for the government to legislate minimum wage. Your staff will reward you ten-fold if you take care of them. Increase your pricing if you need to…. I'd be prepared to pay a higher price if I'm getting exceptional service and quality!

Pretty simple! I'd like to hear from businesses who support their teams. These are the places where I want to take my spending dollars.

Men-Look After Yourself!

Its 4:00 am and Facebook reminded me that two years ago today, I had a major heart attack. How I'm still walking this world amazes me-I should be dead. But, for some reason, I'm still here and plan to be for some time to come. I still have people to piss off and maybe do a little good in this world. I'm not looking for well wishes.... I have an important message to spread.

This post is not meant to be sexist. It has become very clear to me that women do a much better job of taking care of themselves, and in some cases, their families and husbands. We men, to put it bluntly, are a bunch of **dumbasses**. We ignore our bodies, our minds thinking we're the Marvel character Deadpool-we'll heal on our own and don't worry-it'll get better. Rub some dirt on it-it'll go away. It's no big deal, whatever it is. Although whenever we get a cold, we make it seem like death is at our doorsteps-it's weird I know.

I've already told the story about ignoring an infection and losing a leg. Blah blah blah-boring. November 1st, 2016, for the first time in my life, I paid attention to my body. Chest pain struck. A sharp stabbing pain in my chest. I ignored it for a few minutes and continued working. The pain got worse and I collapsed in my wheelchair. Hmmmm, this didn't seem right. I alerted a co-worker, another man, who seemed so nonchalant. He asked if he should call an ambulance and I replied, yeah, maybe you should. While waiting, I collapsed again. EMS showed up quite quickly and I was whisked to University Hospital. I was informed that I had a blocked artery and that I needed a stent. Doctors say I had arrived with very few minutes to spare. One remarked I should have been dead.

Another example of how we men don't look after ourselves has to do with mental health. Dudes my age are taught to hide our feelings- BE A MAN! Suck it up! Wimp! And then, all of a sudden, mid-life crisis happens or we simply, I don't know, try and kill ourselves? We dudes think we're superhuman and nothing should or can beat us down and then, it happens, out of nowhere-we die. This is so preventable and yet we don't pay attention to ourselves until its nearly too late. The lessons I learned from all of this are twofold: 1) I actually enjoy this whole living thing and 2) we're a bunch of selfish bastards. We don't think of the damage and pain we are causing our loved ones.

Throughout my life, I have been surrounded by strong, intelligent and caring women. Each of them has advised me at one time or another about my health. You need to lose weight......when was your last physical.... you should get that looked at.....and each time, I simply ignored it. Even when my foot was so infected, I ignored my partner and let it get so bad that.... well, you know. Why we do this is a mystery to me.

Hindsight is easy. Woulda, coulda, shoulda. Since I can't change the past, I'll try and change the future. No, I'm not some yammering old man- we'll maybe a little. I want the message to men, especially younger men, to be as follows:

- Take care of your body, mentally and physically
- **Listen to the women in your life**- they know what they're talking about!
- Pay attention to signs something may not be alright. Time at the doctor's office is better spent than riding in the back of a screaming ambulance thinking you're going to die
- Imagine the pain you're causing those who love you when you let your health get out of hand.

Most importantly, look after your mental health. Talk to someone you can trust. Cry once in awhile. **HEY-you there rolling your eyes as you read this. Yes you!** Trust me, talking and crying are great. I'm a man, and it took me 50 years to figure this out. For those who judge me for being open-screw you. Don't care. I'm a big boy and I can take it so judge away. I'm here because I listened and did something about it when I knew there was something wrong-both mentally and physically. If not for yourself, do it for your family-they want and need you in their lives.

This is Movember time. This is the first year I will actually participate. I'm finally walking the walk instead of being some jerk who simply talks about it. Funds raised for my campaign will be dedicated to men's mental health. (Link to my site: (https://mobro.co/13831830?mc=1)

I'm still here, annoying the hell out of people thanks to not only the professionals who worked hard to keep me alive, but especially thanks to the caring women in my life. I have a chance to use this time to do some actual good for our neighbours.

To the moms, wives, partners, sisters and friends, I say this: I now listen and will continue to do as I'm told. We men need you more than you know. Your strength keeps us alive. I will never be able to thank you enough. And, dudes-be extra kind to the women in your life. You're probably still on this planet thanks to their caring attitudes.

Here endeth the lesson kids......

Materialism vs Enjoying Life

> "He who dies with the most toys, wins."

These were the words I truly lived by for most of my adult life. Growing up in a single parent family, and the oldest of four kids, we lived a modest life. Old used cars when we had a car, a few toys and refurnished furniture was a way of life. I'm not saying it was a bad way to live, but it was what is was. I still had fun and can't complain.

As a young adult out in the world, I wanted stuff. The first car I ever owned shortly after getting married was a two-toned brown Chevy Chevette. Giant piece of crap, but it got us around town. I bought a band new Panasonic 27" TV and a stereo system to match so that I could watch Star Wars while blowing out the windows. One of my favourite movie lines came from "Wall Street", where Gordon Gecko states: "Greed is Good."

The Chevette gave way to various other flying junkyards, like the used Renault Alliance, a Delta 88 and a Chevy Cavalier. My dream was to own an SUV and I made that dream come true when I bought a used Ford Explorer. I loved that truck and drove it until the transmission died. I then decided it was time for a new car, so off to Ingersoll where I bought my first ever brand-new car, a Chevy Impala. Since then, I always bought new, which was often as I usually put a ton of miles for work and travel.

After buying a house in 1999 in Byron, I bought everything my heart desired. 55" TV, DVD with surround, a new computer, all the toys needed for yard work. I had cable and every bloody conceivable channel you could watch-even the damn Swiss Chalet Channel. I had the money and never went without. I had an impressive DVD collection, wore nice suits to work, always had the latest cell/smart phone. Dining out became a habit versus a treat. Basically, I wanted it, I got it.

I tried to spoil our kids as well. I can't count the number of gaming systems I bought. Not that my kids were demanding- far from it. I wanted to give them what I couldn't have as a kid. When you look back, they would have been happy with a cardboard box. Every year, they'd give me their Christmas wish list and not only would I buy everything on the list, I'd buy more.

Annual vacations to Florida occurred each year, culminating in a very expensive trip to Universal Studios Florida- and when I say expensive, I mean holy hell expensive. But, we made it happen. Have money, will spend.

After my divorce, I set myself up in a new place and spent money on only the best: smart tv, leather furniture, expensive cookware.... everything a newly single dude could want. I probably dined out more than I cooked at this point. I took an expensive trip to Cuba and spared no expense. Costly trips to Toronto, Niagara Falls-wherever I wanted. I bought the best clothes for myself-spoiled myself rotten.

Then, July 9th, 2016 happened, the day I lost my leg. After some consideration, I figured I could no longer drive, so I gave up my car. In September of 2016, I moved into an apartment I couldn't afford. My drinking was way out of hand. And so, on,

April 17th, 2017, life took a dramatic turn. With a long stay on the mental health unit to fix myself up, I was evicted and lost everything. With the exception of a couple of bags of clothes and my laptop, I was reduced to nothing.

Surprisingly, this may have been the greatest thing that ever happened to me! I'm now doing things I should have been doing thirty years ago. I'm exploring London and finding things that I never knew existed in this city- and I've lived her for 41 years! I've started to discover Ontario with trips up north. We Londoners think that we have beautiful fall colours, and we do, but visiting North Bay in October is a sight I've never experienced in my life. I'm growing to love Northern Ontario.

I've, as you've probably noticed, have started writing. Along with this book, I've published my first work of fiction. I'm writing a weekly blog focusing on life, politics, health and any other nonsense I can come up with. I don't have cable anymore. Should have cancelled it years ago. I've become more involved in our community, volunteering, some politics and getting to know the great people in our city.

And you know what? I've never been happier!

Gramma & Poppa and Remembrance Day

As November 11th approaches, its always a good time to reflect on what Remembrance Day means to me. Its pretty simple I suppose-its a day to remember and to be thankful. As a 52-year-old man, I've never been called upon to fight for my country. I have zero lived experience; therefore, I rely on what I have learned from those who fought, survived or died for our freedom, and the freedom for others around the world.

Several members of my family fought in WW1 and WW2. My grandfather, William Walter Briggs, has always been and will always be one of my greatest heroes in the world. Poppa was always a model for the kind of man I wanted to be in this world. I adored my grandfather for a great many reasons. He was a stern man with a serious look on his face. A tall, incredibly strong man, Poppa, in his quiet manner, was a gentle giant.

Poppa was a pilot during WW2. The horrors he must have witnessed or been a part of are something I actually know very little about. Poppa didn't talk about his experiences during the war very much. He'd share some stories, generally about the comradery amongst the other fighting men he encountered. He'd have a smile when he told me the various stories, but when it came to the deadly scenes he witnessed, he would go silent. Once, he started to share a story about a bombing that took place, but then his eyes would well up with tears and he would stop. For his efforts, Poppa was awarded the Distinguished Flying Cross.

Gramma and Poppa returned from the war, married in 1945 and went on to have 8 kids. Poppa had a successful career with Imperial Oil. Both Gramma and Poppa were member s of the Royal Canadian Legion, Victory Branch #317. I was always excited to see my grandparents and was thrilled when we moved here in 1978....closer to my family. I was heartbroken when they would get transferred and then over the moon when they finally moved back. My grandparents were so bloody good to me and I don't think I ever thanked them properly. I love and miss them more than one could imagine.

Bill and Josephine Briggs- My Grandparents

November 11th reminds me to think about what Gramma and Poppa went through, specifically, what they did during the war to ensure the future that I enjoy today. I can say without reservation, the life I enjoy here in Canada are thanks to the sacrifice our veterans made during their time at war. I can vote in a democratic society, speak freely whenever I feel the need and practice whatever lifestyle or religion I chose. I live in a society where intolerance is not acceptable (although this is a battle that still continues), where pot is legal, where business thrives, and our government is not killing its citizens or journalists.

I watch a lot of Anthony Bourdain. His first episode took place in Myanmar. Whenever he spoke with the locals or a local reporter, there was genuine fear, and many wouldn't speak. After decades or government suppression, and even though the times were changing, these citizens still live with the fear that if they speak out of line, the government will imprison them. The random footage of the towns and cities shows a population that isn't living a life filled with happiness. They looked downtrodden and scared. In another episode set in Singapore, Bourdain sits down with three young people over a meal. Even though they seemed content and happy, I could still see some reservation when they spoke about their city. We don't have to endure that here in Canada.

Here in Canada, we live in relative peace and tranquility. I won't for one moment deny that we don't have our share of social and political issues. We have homelessness, mental health and addiction epidemics. We argue about transit and whether or not it's too early to put up Christmas decorations. We shoot our mouths off on social media and bitch about gas prices. We complain about the lineups at drive-thrus and spend weeks trying to figure out what to dress up as for

Halloween. Putting things into perspective, some of the things we complain about are rather petty and minor, considering the bigger issues we face and given what many others around the world are going through.

But what I am most proud of is that our veterans fought to protect those who couldn't protect themselves. Throughout our existence, Canada has continually went to where the danger was to ensure the safety of people who needed our help. Our military and peacekeepers are respected for their work. In the last century, brave men and women have not only protected and fought for us but stood up against evil that people around the world have endured.

Seeing veterans fighting to get the benefits they are entitled to makes me incredibly angry. We as a country enjoy the freedoms that we do today thanks to these incredibly brave people- can we not at least give them everything that they deserve? This should be a no-brainer yet here we are, November 2018 and our government continues to not support and care for the citizens who protected us.

I am grateful beyond words to not only our amazing veterans who, in many cases, gave their lives, but to everyone who continues to serve. If you're in the military full time or as a reserve- thank you. You are the true heroes in our world.

And to Gramma and Poppa: I miss you. I love you. And thank you.

Dudes-Keep it in Your Pants!

While watching the Nov 6th American election results, a tweet popped up announcing that Conservative MP Tony Clement was resigning from his numerous roles on federal committees due to a sexting scandal and extortion attempt. After checking multiple news outlets to confirm, my first thought was "what in the hell was he thinking-he couldn't be that stupid!" Apparently, he is that stupid. Like so many folks, I have opinions.

Forget that Clement is a public figure for a moment. I'm wondering what motivates a man to want to send pictures of his junk. If you do feel the need, why send them to someone you don't really know or trust. In my career as a manager, I had to terminate someone for doing the exact same thing. First of all, the person he sent them to did not want them. He used a company phone. He sent them during work. I was stunned at the time-what the hell motivated him to behave like this?

I saw a tweet that posed the question-do all men think with their dick? This may be true I suppose. We dudes seem to behave in a manner of ways that most can't comprehend. But in the end, there is zero excuse for this behaviour. There can be an argument to be made that what happens on our own time is our own business....and I agree with this. Hey, you want to be a pothead at home or be pervert at home and your behaviour doesn't affect others, that's your business and I could care less. But when your behaviour creeps into the public and involves innocent people, people that don't want this type of activity in their lives, then we have a problem.

If Clement did this on his own time and it involved consenting adults, I'd have no problem with this. But it is very clear that this was not the case. What stuns me is that he, as an intelligent adult, fell for this bloody scheme. Its 2018, haven't we seen time and time again where people fall for scams? And as a public figure, you'd have to think he'd be a target? Doesn't anyone remember Anthony Weiner? And, again, given it's 2018, have we not learned to trust literally no one? Ask the Ottawa Senators players caught yammering on about their coach in an Uber about not thinking and trusting. Even if this was an extortion plan, how can you completely trust a spurned lover. Ever heard of revenge porn?

What I found somewhat weird were the number of people feeling sorry for Clement. Are you kidding me?? He, as a grown man, did this to himself. He chose to send texts with pictures of his junk. I feel terrible for his family, his friends and his working team. This is a humiliating incident. And I get the sense that this may devastate his family for some time to come. I feel zero sympathy for Clement....... I'll explain.

This act committed by Clement is disgusting-there is no denying that. However, history has shown that public figures who act inappropriately in this manner, or those who engage in an affair, can and are forgiven. Bill Clinton rings a bell. Hear me out for a second before slamming your smartphone down. Our current mayor, soon to be leaving office, didn't resign nor did I think he should. Yes, trust is lost, and the voters would have had something to say about that had he run again. His partner, who knowingly took part in the affair, ran for office and won her seat again. Forgive and move on is my thought. People make mistakes and we McJudgies love to jump on the bandwagon and want these people destroyed.

In Clement's case, I agree he should step down. It is clear that this wasn't just a case of sending explicit photos- a check of his

Instagram account it appears he's creeping young women. This is intolerable and absolutely disgusting. I have absolutely no understanding why people behave on social media the way they do....no clue. Seemingly intelligent people, specifically men, who, for some reason, feel the need to behave in such a slimy manner is incomprehensible to me. I have a 21-year-old daughter and if he or any other scumbag did this to her, you can sure there'd be a major ass kicking-even with my prosthetic leg.

We hold public officials to a much higher standard and in most cases, we should. But, if we are to judge, we need to look at each incident separately. People make mistakes and quite frankly, will pay for these mistakes dearly. Our judgement doesn't help. And to be honest, in some cases, its none of our damn business. But some people are simply d-bags. Clement, who I thought was actually a decent politician, falls into the d-bag category.

The bigger issue that is troubling, well, very disturbing, is the continued sexual harassment of the women in our community. This behaviour hasn't been condoned or acceptable well, since forever. Even with all the scandals, workplace harassment, stalking and other disgusting activities, have we not learned anything yet or are we just plain stupid, ignorant or arrogant. I was raised by incredibly strong women and I was never taught to behave like this. If I had acted in this manner, my mother, grandmother and, the scariest of the bunch, **my mother in law would have kicked the literal crap out of me.** The companies I worked for taught us, on many many......many occasions the importance of professional and respectful behaviour. As a society, we have watched the various scandals in Hollywood take place with disgust. The **#metoo** movement has shown that we have a long way to go to ensure a society free from harassment and assault. Just a few days ago, Conservative MPP Jim Wilson "resigned" due to sexual misconduct allegations. When will we ever learn?

Having said all of this, not all men act in this deplorable manner. There are many great men out there in our world. Please don't paint an entire segment of our population with one brush. We're not all pigs. The lessons learned, and its sort of pathetic that these lessons still need to be taught, are as follows: a) don't trust social media, b) stop trusting people who haven't earned the trust and c) act like adults and behave. We're adults- not a bunchy of horny teenagers.

And oh yeah, keep your junk in your pants guys......its just simply disgusting.

Losing My Religion

I can't pinpoint the exact day, but I know exactly when I decided to move away from organized religion, specifically the Catholic Church. Give me a few minutes, I'll get there, I promise.

I was born and raised as a Catholic. My earliest memories in the church took place in Oakville Ontario, at, I think it was St. Andrew's Church. I was a young alter boy at an Italian church led by Father Pucci. When we moved to London, we started to attend St. Pius X Church in Oakridge and I continued as an alter boy. I was surprised as we had female servers as well, something I didn't see in Oakville.

The parish priest, Father Joseph Schneider, was an amazing community leader and priest. When I started at Catholic Central High, we were required to do a day of service and Father Joe would have a bunch of us come and do a fall clean up at the church. As I was about to enter grade 11 at CCH, my mother couldn't afford the tuition-we had to pay in those days to go to a Catholic high school. Father Joe sponsored me, and I was able to continue at CCH.

After moving to the east end in 1983, our family switched to St. Patrick's on Dundas and Ashland, which had a remarkable priest in Father Tremblay. And again, I served as an alter boy. After leaving home, I stopped going to church and changed to a public high school. This wasn't a conscious decision, it just happened.

Prior to getting married, we were required to attend Marriage Prep courses. For several weeks, we were taught the Catholic way in marriage. Complete and utter waste of time. But, of course, being Catholic and marrying a Catholic, the ceremony took place at the beautiful and historical St. Peters Basilica, with Father Tony Daniels officiating.

Two kids and two baptisms later, I was still attending mass again, but really to satisfy my wife and to be a role model to my kids. I didn't receive communion as I felt I was breaking a commandment by not honouring my father and mother. After a conversation with Father Bob Remark back at St. Pius, I was absolved and continued to attend church.

I guess the wheels fell off when I was attending a mass at St. George's in Byron. During the homily, Father Gary went on to scold parents who brought their small children to mass who were disruptive. He felt that parents who brought their small ones and the little snacks, like a baggie of Cheerios to keep them occupied was completely disrespectful.

Now, in principle, I suppose he may have been correct. However, after listening to one sermon after another whether the church preached family and community, then to turn around and publicly criticize young parents was somewhat hypocritical in my mind. I was already questioning the church at this point, and this was the final push out the door.

I'm not going to get into the numerous sex scandals that have occurred in the Catholic Church. These heinous acts continue even today and enough has been written about them. This is one of the main reasons I left the church, but its only one among many.

I understand tradition. Thousands of years of writings and teachings cannot be dismissed. But here's the thing: this isn't working anymore. Congregations are shrinking, and people are either questioning their faith and simply leaving the church as I did. The Catholic Church as failed, in my humble opinion, to simply keep up with the times. Here are some areas where the church has not kept up with our faced paced, world changing pace:

- Male only priests. I have never liked the imbalance between men and women. Priests live in nice condos, yet nuns live in poverty. Women are still not equal in the church.
- Unmarried priests: I find it odd that an unmarried faith leader stands before us to preach about the value of a family. If we let priests marry and have a family, its my sense this lived experience would prove to be very valuable. I know we now have married Deacons, but this is not the same.
- I believe in birth control for many reasons, yet the church wants to continue to push abstinence.
- The continued unacceptance of the gay community. Same sex relationships have existed since time began, yet the Catholic Church continues to shun a portion of our population.

I'm not against religion nor am I saying I don't believe in God. Every religion has some wonderful teachings that, in the end, teach us to be a better people. Whether you are Islamic, Buddhist, Anglican or a Jedi, we can all agree that these houses of worship can and do teach us what it means to be a caring, community minded human. If following your religion is what is needed to bring peace to your mind and our world, then I'm all for it, I respect, and I am appreciative of your efforts.

The Catholic Church needs to recognize that it needs to change and regain the trust they have lost from so many of their followers. The are numerous articles that can be found that illustrate a significant decline in attendance in the Catholic parishes. Here in London, churches have closed, and congregations have been combined. If the Catholic leadership continue their rather stubborn resistance to change, their faithful followers will continue to disappear.

The Women in My Life

I'm a 52-year-old man, well educated and somewhat well versed in the world. I know sexism has existed since, well, forever. I've always been aware and have been against discrimination against women since the day I was born. Let me tell you why.

I was born into a female dominated family. My father left when I was very young, and my mother was thrust into the world of single parenting. My mother was the victim of severe male abuse, both physically and mentally. I can recall several moments in my childhood where my mother would scoop up her four kids and make a run for it due to the violence she faced. My father and her subsequent partner were violent alcoholics.

Moving to London in 1978, we were now living in a city close to my grandparents. My grandmother was a strong woman and again, the head of the family. My mother worked full time and due to her work ethic, was elevated to the position of General Manager- a considerable feat considering the fact that she worked in a male dominated facility. We were taught as kids to never raise your hands to a woman. My mother, Lucy, was an incredibly strong woman who could do anything a man could do. For a short period, I lived with my grandparents. As I said, Gramma was the head of the family. My aunts, all five of them, were incredibly strong and independent women. To put it bluntly, they didn't take any crap from any man.

I married a very strong and brilliant woman, and by doing so, I gained a mother-in-law. Let me tell you something, you didn't mess with this little five-foot-nothing woman from Newfoundland. She was a very strong woman who not only raised four kids but worked full time and maintained her independence. Phyllis had a strong influence in my life, and not only did I love her to death, but I respected the hell out of her.

Entering the work world, I was employed at Western University. Most of my supervisory team were incredible, female leaders. Smart, hard working treated their staff with support and dignity. I worked with several female managers who worked circles around most of us. Our Associate Vice-President was a woman, as were the AVP's of Human and Resources and Finance. The Vice President was a terrific leader....and was a woman. All of these amazing women wanted and deserved equality and respect......the same things that male leaders seemed to automatically receive simply for being a man.

And then there is my buddy ole pal Nadine. An incredibly talented chef, Nadine has built a 25-year career in what is traditionally a man's world. Having worked in the finest restaurants, culminating in being appointed the first female Executive Chef at the Western Fair, Nadine exemplified what a true leader is to her team. What was disappointing and quite frankly, unforgivable, was that the company who employed her, (**NOT the Fair**,) decided to pay her significantly less than her predecessor. Nadine transformed the culinary department yet was worth less than the previous guy, who was a disaster I might add. What the hell??

During the recent provincial and municipal elections, a number of strong female candidates emerged. And this is when I was reminded once again of the inequality in our world. These magnificent candidates were subjected to sexism, discrimination and violent threats. Each of these fine folks faced this kind of ignorance with pure professionalism and grace. Given these circumstances, I'm not sure I would have reacted in this manner.

When I look back at our political past, its easy to come up with a list of female politicians that I respect and admire, but not so much when it come to male leaders. Not to say that some men have not been great leaders, such as Obama or Jack Layton, but our female leaders tend to be less controversial and more professional. I think of names like Joni Baechler, Peggy Sattler, Tanya Park and Irene Mathysson to name a few.

As I was writing this, I was thinking of other role models in my world and it was easy to come up with a number of examples of where a woman has had a positive effect on my life yet, until now, I didn't think of them as women. My family doctor, a doctor who has taken the time to get to know me and my medical history, who is always prepared with up to date info if I was in the hospital, knows me inside and out. Dr Sargo, a female, may be the best doctor I've ever had. When I was in trouble with addiction, every single professional I dealt with on my road to recovery was a woman. When dealing with them, the last thing I was thinking was that they were female.... I only thought of them as professionals.

And then once again, three times in the last week, male politicians have found themselves in a world of trouble over sexual harassment, sexting and bullying. I am astounded when I shouldn't be. This disgusting behaviour continues to occur, no matter what. Creeping young women on Instagram, sending pictures of one's man parts and other repulsive behaviour continues to occupy some men's mind. Are we that arrogant and moronic that we feel we have the right or the need to subject woman to this......seemingly on a daily basis?

In June 2010, Bill 168 was passed which legislated a safer work environment, free from bullying and harassment. Employers are required by law to educate and train their employees on an annual basis to ensure they conduct themselves in a professional manner that maintains a safe work environment. Here we are, almost 9 years later and this continues to be a workplace concern.

The absolute worst scenarios continue to be played out each and every day: violence against women. Each day, women suffer physical and mental abuse at the hands of a man. In my opinion, our laws are nowhere near tough enough to deter or punish those who commit these acts. Back in my working days, years ago, the daughter of one of my staff was brutally murdered by a boyfriend. The piece of crap killer was ordered to stay away from her, yet this didn't deter him from committing murder of a young beautiful mom. Last week, a London police officer was released after failing to adhere to terms of release, not just once, but multiple times. Is there a chance he'll violate these terms again-I'd bet the house on it. Our laws are simply not strong enough!!!! Despite the efforts of great organizations like the London Abused Women's Centre and the ongoing lobbying, our governments continue to resist stepping up the fight to eliminate violence against women.

In April 2018, a man in a van in Toronto runs down and kills 10 people and injures 15. News reports that the casualties were predominately women. This murdered was a self proclaimed "Incel", a term referring to involuntary celibate. From what was gathered, many "Incels" belong to various message boards and target their inability to engage in intimate relationships with women. Many Incels are known to target their wrath on women. What in the holy hell? Due to their pathetic personal inadequacies, they target woman?? I don't get it.... I really don't. What kind of sick, demented men are these people?

Historically, sexism has existed forever, and I get that. But given that we are now approaching the year 2019, how is it that our society has yet to fully embrace equality? I can't speak for anyone else, but both personally and professionally, I was taught to treat everyone as equals. This leaves me wondering not only why sexism still continues but how do we level the playing field. For me personally, this means that I will continue to stand up against the double standards we see and ensure that I am an ally in this on-going struggle. I need to stand beside these brave women, show my support and say, "I WILL NOT TOLERATE THIS!" I need to push out law makers to make this issue a top priority.

To the dumbass men who protest when, say, a local restaurant offers a discount to women on Mondays, or offers a lady's night, shut your mouth. You only make yourself look like a moron and quite frankly, none of us want to hear this nonsense. Women have been treated like second class, underpaid citizens for far too long and its about time they get what is owed to them. And if anyone wants to shoot their mouth off over this column, don't bother. I don't have time for any of your verbal diarrhea so piss off.

To all the women not only in my life, but in our world, I say this: Thank you for your leadership and guidance. I cannot apologize enough that you have to face this kind of adversity. Keep up the fight and your hard work. There are a great many men who have your back.

The Art of Grocery Shopping

Many of us have a love-hate relationship with the weekly trip to the grocery store. Whether its No-Frills, Superstore or Metro, the task of picking up the weekly supplies can be a giant pain in the ass. My pal Nadine and I sat down and thought about the different type of shoppers we encounter. Some make us chuckle, others-not so much.

The List Maker: Many of us sit down and make the list of what we need. I'm one of those who forgets the list and have to wing it. When I actually remember the damn thing, there's always the issue of thinking you've finished the shopping only to discover you missed something, and that something is generally on the other side of the store. I guess the solution is to create a list in the order of the departments you need to grab a product from? Who the hell has that much time of organizational skills?

The Label Reader: You know what I'm talking about-the dreaded label reader who makes a point of checking every ingredient, sugar or fat content on the label, thereby blocking your access to the shelf. In some cases, reading the label is important-nut allergies, sugar content etc. I get it. The issue is that in many cases, the shopper already knows what's in the food item. Get the hell out of the way would ya!

Impulse Purchases-Treats: Damn those tasty treats you find in the middle of the aisles or at the checkouts. You sneak a treat or two unto the check out conveyor and inevitably think you're getting the judgemental look from the cashier. How many of us, after placing the Gummy Bears or Reese's Pieces on the belt, got the look and said they were for the kids? Come on….be honest! You can't BS me……I've done it.

The Obstacle Course: Speaking of the treats in the middle of the aisle, and I get why they do it, but I wish stores would quit putting the temporary displays and racks in the aisles. Tough enough maneuvering around the label readers, socializers and the shelf stockers. Sometimes I feel I should appear on the American Ninjas show as I've become quite adept to the rigors of crazy obstacles.

The Screaming/Pooping Kids: I've got two kids, both grown up now-thank god. But we've all had that one kid who decides that the middle of the shopping trip is when they either have some sort of meltdown or decide to have the stinkiest poop. My son always chose the latter....and seemed damn proud of it every time.

The Snooty Wanderer: You know exactly who I am talking about. The dolt with the Starbucks in one hand, trying to push the cart with the other while texting on their phone......this breeds the ⬇

Grocery Road Rager: I can certainly be labelled a rager. Stuck behind the person with the Starbucks or the group of four that seem to walk in a row instead of one behind each other. We tend to avoid the grocery store on weekends and Mondays.

Cart or Basket: You think you're just going to run in and grab a few things, so you pick up one of those small baskets on the way in. Turns out you choose more than you thought and try and manage the arm load like a Las Vegas juggler.

Tag Team Shopping: Shopping as a couple, you realize you forgot mushrooms in the produce section and tell your partner you'll grab them and that you'll meet her near the registers.

You return to the registers and find your partner, but she doesn't have the grocery cart because she thought you took it. It's a long walk trying to find your abandoned cart.

The Shopping Bags: Overall, I think shoppers do a good job collecting and trying to re-use the reusable grocery bags. You know the ones I'm talking about-the ones you realize you left in the back seat just as you're checking out. That'll be fifty cents please for the plastic bags you have to buy. Oh well, they make great kitty litter bags.

The Selfish, Lazy Shopper: Probably my biggest pet peeve. We're talking about that A-hole who leaves their empty coffee cup on a shelf instead of putting it in the garbage. But what is worse, is the completely selfish and ignorant jerkoff who grabs something, say a package of meat, and decides they don't want it. So, instead of putting it back where they got it, they dump it on any shelf. These are the same dipshits who complain about rising prices.

Price Matchers-Points Collectors: I get trying to save a buck or two. Its smart and sensible. But for the love of all that is holy, do you need to flip through your phone for every bloody item to save a dime? Come on. You're also the same person who has every known points collection app yet always seem surprised when they ask-then spend time flipping through all the apps on your phone.

The Snacker: These are the people whose fingers I'd like to break. Testing or eating foods before actually paying for the product-what the hell?

Tag Team Shopping Part Two: The couple, usually a little older, who shop together. They're easy to recognize. The male is the bored looking one while the female, the smarter of the two, is taking her time ensuring the best price and value is chosen. Unlike the male shopper, like me, who can rack up $200 in ten minutes flat as we throw whatever we like, despite the price into the car. We're also the guy who spent the $200 and yet only carries in three bags.

<u>Getting Home:</u> I suppose this comes from the fact that as a rule, we're lazy. We're the ones who arrive home with the groceries and try and carry all 11 bags in at once. We're the ones who have the ends of our fingers with the blood circulation cut off. I would suggest we turn this into an Olympic sport because I think most of us dudes think that grocery bag carrying is a feat of strength.

<u>Tag Team Shopping Part Three:</u> I admit it, I'm one of these guys. Yes-I'm guilty okay! I'm the partner who, when their better half isn't looking, slips that bag or two of Doritos into the cart. Your partner discovers this when its too late as she unloads the cart while you do the bagging. We've all gotten that "you sneaky bastard" look.

<u>Single Guy Shopping:</u> On that rare occasion when you live the single life, say, when your partner is out of town and you've got the place to yourself for a few days. Nothing like Swanson TV Dinners, meat pies and fries, or a good package of hotdogs, a bag of corn chips and a bottle of pop to tide you over. Problem is getting rid of the stuff before the smarter half gets home.

<u>The Grocery Bagger</u>: Remember back when grocery stores had staff that bagged your groceries? Now, we self bag and it feels like a time trial sport to bag your food as fast as humanly

possible before the next person's groceries start making their way down the conveyor.

<u>The Total Contest:</u> We all do it, try and guesstimate the total you spent like we're contestants on The Price is Right. I used to be damn good at it, but lately, Nadine seems to be kickass at it.

That's my fun take on grocery shopping. Now, don't even get me started about shopping at Walmart.

Homelessness: Solutions and Costs

I have to state right upfront that I am by no means an expert. Other than my own experience with mental illness and near homelessness, and from what I have read and watched, I have little education these issues. But I had a thought.

I watched an episode on Parts Unknown filmed in Singapore. Before I continue, I'm sure that Singapore's solution is not perfect and I'm only seeing one side of the story. Singapore does have a homeless problem, to deny this would be inaccurate. Begging is illegal so there may not be as many homeless on street corners or in front of stores. There are social housing projects in place that the government manages, and charges rent based on income. Many homeless can be found on the beaches, airports or outside the cities. The government's approach is at least a start but it's far from perfect.

I guess given the fact that I'm not living in my former life of luxury in Byron, and by my own design, ignored the social problems that existed, I'm seeing more and more homelessness and mental illness issues out on our streets. Downtown, on Oxford St, in front of every store and in the middle of the roads. During the summer, I was spending weekends downtown and was seeing first hand the number of homeless sleeping on the streets, in door ways and in the back of parking lots. In the summer of 2017, I saw many camping in the park in the trees in Carfrae Park. A walk along the TVP behind London Hydro revealed many more living in the woods.

So, I got to thinking. Forget about the financial cost for the moment. I'd like to see a complex built for those that are homeless and have mental issues and/or addiction issues. Here is my plan:

A two-building complex consisting of two high-rises:

The first building, consisting of bachelor and one-bedroom units that gets people out of the cold/heat and gets them started on the road to re-building their lives. If they qualify for OW/ODSP, the rent portion they receive goes directly to the group managing these facilities. Occupants are limited to a six-month timetable. Here, they are required to get the assistance they need, such as addictions therapy, mental health treatment. A permanent safe injections site is also located on the premises. A walk-in clinic is set up to assist with daily health issues, i.e.: flu shots...same as what you'd receive with a family doctor. Life skills are taught/refreshed such as budgeting, cooking on a budget etc. If job retraining is required for those capable of working, then these services are accessed. Resume building and job searching begins, working with partner companies. If one is not able to work, suggest volunteering on the property, i.e.: upkeep, minor maintenance, cooking in community kitchen. If the person is then ready to tackle the world, they are then transferred to.......

Building 2: Potentially, a permanent place of residence. Again, bachelors and one bedrooms, with rents geared to either support or income. Residents can still access services in building one, such as an AA group, addictions support groups, computer access and so on. Residents must have completed the transitional services in building one.

Now, the cost. I have zero idea as to what it would cost to build and maintain. And this is the root of the problem when tackling these issues: where does the money come from? I get the sense that many who have opinions on this issue, like me, either don't understand that there is a cost and the question as to who pays. Some give a damn about the cost-just get it done. This isn't a reasonable line of thinking as money does play into this. Let's pretend it will cost $100 million to build and set up this complex. Is it reasonable to suggest that all three levels of government kick in 1/3 of the cost? Then we need to build an annual budget to manage the facility- heat, hydro, water, staffing, maintenance and so on. The rent charged to the tenants/clients in need won't cover it. We then need to find these funds, or do we privatize?

The next troubling issue are the terms "gentrification" and "NIMBYism", two terms that I absolutely detest, however they are real concerns. Typically, gentrification refers to the transformation of an area to suit the needs and wants of the middle class. With the desire to improve downtown, some may be resistant to either opening a business or patronizing downtown due to the presence of the street folk. If we provide these people in dire need of a helping hand, maybe the process of working the two projects hand in hand (downtown and a complex for those in need), then we eliminate the accusations of gentrification? Then there are the NIMBY people. How do we manage their concerns? Where do we build such a facility to appease the citizens yet still make it accessible?

As we consider the long-term solutions, the priority needs to be the short term-how do we get these vulnerable people out of the cold, get food in their stomachs and help with the challenges they face? There are far more intelligent people than me who continue to devote their efforts to this crisis-people who have actually come up with solutions. The problem reverts back to money. All three levels of governments need to recognize that this is a crisis that many cities across our country are faced with. This isn't just a London problem, but from what I'm seeing, London seems to have a much bigger challenge than many other cities. We as the voters need to challenge our government officials to put homelessness and mental health on the top of their priority list.

I may be ridiculously naïve when I say this, but my sense is that if we can solve/reduce/eliminate/assist with these challenges, we will not only create a better society, but, for the fiscally focused citizens, we may actually save some money. A look at London's crime stats map is showing, in the last month, a high number of break-ins, thefts and robberies taking place. Even recently, one of the city's Kindness Meters was stolen-again. Is this happening because people are thieving bastards or because people are so desperate for money for drugs, alcohol or food, that they turn to crime? I suspect a bit of both. But, if those in need had a place to go, would the crime stats go down? If crime is reduced, the less money we spend on policing? I was the victim of several thefts from my car and my apartment and I've often wondered what the motivation was to lead someone to do this. I always hoped it was because the thieves were in such dire straits that they behaved like this- but I am also a realist and understand that some do commit crimes simply because they are thieving bastards.

Now think about health care costs. As has been demonstrated by the good people at the Middlesex London Health Unit and Dr. Mackie, the opening of safe injection sites not only prevents overdoses, but cleaner tools (needles for example) that helps prevent the spread of HIV and Hepatitis. This is a most cost-effective method than treating those who are exposed. Again, saving lives and saving money? I believe so. However, a feasibility study would either prove or disprove my theory.

By building a facility like the one I described above, its quite possible that in the long run, not only would it be more cost effective, but far more importantly, lives are saved.

Board Games- Should I Go Professional?

I like board games. Trivial Pursuit, Scrabble and Monopoly to name a few. I used to own multiple copies of Trivial Pursuit and even had the Star Wars version of Monopoly. Before I continue, there are things about me that some of you may not know.

I'm competitive. I'm arrogant. I have some sort of "Rain Man" ability to retain useless information, knowledge and trivia. I may have forgotten what the Pythagorean Theory was in school or forget to put pants on some days, but I can certainly quote you music lyrics, oddball trivia and movie facts-too bad I couldn't make a living from it. Some have tried to convince me to go on Jeopardy or Who Wants to be a Millionaire.

When I worked, I was competitive. I always tried to be better at everything. Once in a while, I'm reminded that I'm not the best. Once, during my Domino's days, I thought I was a superstar pizza maker until a friend smoked me one day during a competition. In my best days though, I can still bang out a large pepperoni in less than a minute. Competition in the workplace is a good thing at times-gets your team's blood flowing as they try and kick the boss's ass.

As a father, I was absolutely competitive, especially with my son Phillip. There was no way I'd ever let him beat me at anything. That was until I tried to play videos games with the little pecker and he clean my clock. I did beat him-once-while playing Guitar Hero. Once, when I was coaching his soccer team, I tried to play in a pickup game with my team. Not only did Phillip run circles around me, but the near heart attack gave me moment of pause. Phillip still loves to remind me that I can't skate backwards on the ice. Jerk.

So, I'm competitive and back to the board games. I love Trivial Pursuit-every single version of the game. I can only remember once or twice when I didn't win. Whether it's the original version, Pop Culture or Star Wars, I usually do well. Scrabble is the same-I do very well.

Now, Monopoly, a game where the winner is the person who basically bankrupts their competitors. Some suggest that a good game of Monopoly could/should take hours. Lots of strategy is involved. I call BS- my aggressive nature means to play to win and quickly dispensing of your opponents. I don't lose that often.

The challenge is to find people to play with! My buddy ole pal gets quite pissed at my competitive nature and after some reflection, maybe I am too aggressive. In life, in games, I play to win. Many a game has ended prematurely when the odds of winning by my opponent quickly dwindles. I do remember one time spending quite some time picking up Scrabble pieces.

I refuse to "let the other win". This is not my nature. When I do something, I try and give it my full effort. Having said that, I've come to the realization that I need to slow it down. Too many have picked up their ball and have gone home.

So…. anyone want to play a game?

Christmas Craziness

Oh, its Christmas time. The silly season. Possibly one of the most enjoyable yet most stressful times of the year. For some, it can be downright depressing. The last three years, and being divorced, I tried to ignore Christmas, failed, and couldn't wait for all of this nonsense to end. This year, I'm going to enjoy the season as I used to enjoy the holidays quite a bit. With younger kids, I guess it was much easier and enjoyable.

I thought it was prudent to take a moment of pause before diving into the madness that is Christmas to not only think of past Christmases, but how to ensure a more enjoyable holiday season where the stresses of the past are at least minimized. I'm not going to even touch the religious aspect of the season but explore a few ideas as to how to make the next few weekends pleasurable.

In the past, budget was not a concern for me. The past couple of years, given my circumstances, my spending is very limited. I used to panic because I was unable to buy gifts for those that I loved. I'm not being selfish when I say this, but I can't worry about this anymore. I do my best-and those who love and care for me completely understand. If you're in a position where this is a concern for you and you are made to feel guilty by some, consider re-thinking your circle of "loved ones."

This is a great time of need for many. Many organizations are out there asking for our support-support they desperately need in order to serve those who are struggling. It's not reasonable to financially support them all, and don't feel ashamed if you can't give as much or any at all. If this a true concern for you, maybe volunteer a few hours of your time instead. Volunteers are always needed; your time is greatly appreciated, and you'll be surprised as to how rewarding the experience was for you! What an awesome way to give of yourself.

This can be a lonely and sad time for some. Take a moment to check in or visit with some of these people who just need a little social companionship. A gift of your time and friendship lasts a very long time.

Its now time to hit the malls and stores- something many dread. Each year, it seems the parking lots get crazier, meaner and downright frustrating. Don't bother trying to find the closest parking spot. Its not worth the aggravation. Consider taking the bus, or not shop during those ridiculous busy times. If you do drive, London Police are already reminding driving to not leave your purchases, purses, bags etc. out in the open. The light-fingered thieves are out there in full force.

Exercise some patience and a little gratitude to the retail workers of the world. The busiest time of the year can be relentlessly busy, and these incredible workers are working overtime to ensure a good customer service. Please treat them with respect and I don't know, say thank you once in awhile?

The office Christmas parties are now in full swing. During my days at the Western Fair District, our team, on a Friday and Saturday, would cater to a thousand guests a day at the various parties. Our culinary team would work insane hours, cooking more turkey than I thought was possible. The servers and bartenders would put a ton of miles on their shoes and the poor dish guys would work into the wee hours of the morning getting ready for the next day. I encourage you to enjoy-they work hard to make your event great. But don't be an ass to them. I can't tell you then number of moronic drunk guests we've had to toss. Don't be that one guy everyone talks about Monday morning-you know that guy-gets drunk, tries to create a ruckus and pick a fight with the boss. Don't be him.

If you do plan on enjoying the egg nogs with the spiced rum or a few Christmas doobies, plan a ride home BEFORE you go out. MADD Canada/London and their Red Ribbon campaign are in full swing. RIDE Programs will be in place. Don't risk the lives of others-or yourself, because you're an inconsiderate d-bag. LTC, cabs, UBER and companies who will drive your car home are at your service to ensure a safe holiday season. Each year, we hear of people being killed or injured due to impaired drivers. Be nice to have a season where we don't hear about this at all. No excuses.

Take some time to relax and enjoy yourself. Whatever it takes for you to have peace of mind, do it! I love to cozy up and watch some seasonal favourites. Can't beat Christmas Vacation (Holy shit-where's the Tylenol), Scrooged or the 1951 black and white version of a Christmas Carol starring Alistair Sim. A good laugh or a feel-good story is a great way to make you smile and cure the seasonal blues. A little cousin Eddie can go a long way!

One of the best parts of the holidays is the food! There can never be enough turkey, dressing/stuffing and all the fixings. I posted this on Twitter the other day and it seems like I'm in the minority, but I LOVE Christmas Fruitcake, Plum Pudding and Mincemeat treats. Nothing- and I mean nothing celebrates the holidays like an overdose of turkey and Christmas cake followed by a nap. Back in the good old days (did I really just say that?), my Grandmother would go all out with Christmas baking. There was never a shortage of sausage rolls, shortbread cookies and pies- I mean more pies that you could imagine. The menu had to include pumpkin pie covered with so much whipped cream, you never saw the actual pie. This is followed by days of turkey leftovers. Hot turkey, turkey salad sandwiches, turkey soup, turkey casserole, turkey tetrazzini.... turkey.... turkey....turkey. So much turkey that you didn't want to see another bird until the following the following Thanksgiving. My point being-overindulge once a year and enjoy it!!!

Elvis. Yes, Elvis Presley. This may sound really dorky, but I love Elvis Christmas music. Its weird, I know. I'm not a fan of the 24 hours of Christmas music that starts in, oh, I don't know, July, that some radio stations play. I can't stand a lot of the modern takes on holiday music. You know what I'm talking about- the remakes by every so-called singer who completely destroy the classics. Yep-love me some Burl Ives, Nat King Cole and Elvis. I even love a little Annie Lennox, Bing Crosby and the silly songs in the older 60's and 70's Christmas cartoons. But if I hear Mariah Carey or "Do They Know its Christmas" by Band Aid one more time......I'll lose it. Okay Gerry, settle down and get back on track.

I discovered that the great people in the Philippines start celebrating Christmas in September while watching a Parts Unknown episode. What made me smile, and tear up once or twice, was the happiness, joy and celebration that they enjoy. The smiles on the faces of family at big family gatherings are priceless.

At the end of the day, I encourage everyone to slow down a little, enjoy your loved ones, eat way too many treats, have a 'nog or two and make your holiday season one filled with smiles, hugs and fun, while limiting the stress. Stay safe......and........Merry Christmas!

Aging and Legacy

Now that I'm in a somewhat forced retirement at the age of 52, I have the time to not only reflect on the past, but what does my remaining future look like. I remember was I was 13 or 14, I kept thinking about what life and the world would look like when I turned 34 in the year 2000. Now, in 2018, I'm spending probably more time than I should pondering the past.

There are many "coulda, woulda, shoulda" moments. What could I have done differently or what would I have changed? Oh sure, there are moments that I think of that I probably should have made differently and made much better choices. Like the time in 1989, while cutting grass, I slid down a hill and my foot slipped under a lawnmower. This was the start of a path that I believe led to me ultimately losing my leg 27 years later. But, in the end, my past is what has made me the person I am today-good and not so good. My friend Michael continually reminds me that "there is no future in the past" and he's quite right.

In the past few weeks, I've tried to change my thinking from my past to not only what my future looks like, but what will my legacy look like when I'm gone. This isn't morbid thinking-its an effort to ensure that the footprint I left on this world is a positive legacy. The "he who dies with the best toys wins" is probably not the best epitaph. No one writes "she was a great boss" on their tombstone.

My mindset about thinking of my remaining future continues to be at the forefront of my brain right now every time someone passes away. No, I'm not one of the dudes with the magnifying glass checking out the obituaries. This past week, Stan Lee passed away. Most know who Stan was, but for those who don't, he was the creator of many of the comic book heroes I not only enjoyed growing up, but in movies today. Iron Man, Thor, Doctor Strange and Spiderman to name a few. For a few moments, I was obviously sad to see Mr. Lee pass away, but then my thoughts turned to what he left behind. His cameos in the many Marvel movies were generally funny, but the comics and the movies are still here for us to enjoy over and over again. They bring us entertainment and happiness.

John Candy left us in 1994, yet even today, we enjoy his movies, his humor and his life in our world. Who doesn't chuckle whenever the words "Uncle Buck" are mentioned? Carrie Fisher died in late 2016. The memories she left, not only as Princess Leia, but her wicked sense of humour and the wisdom that she shared while battling addiction and struggling with Bi-Polar Disorder were such gifts that she would leave behind.

Think of the music left behind by John Lennon, Elvis and Beethoven. Songs and amazing instrumental pieces that we continue to enjoy to this day. They left indelible marks on our lives, many of them piquing our imagination and inspiring future generations of artists and musicians. That's one heck of a legacy to leave behind. Now, back to a little reality, none of us are celebrities-well maybe one or two of you are-but most of us are not. However, it is possible to leave a mark or two on this world before our time on earth comes to an end.

I've attended many funerals and at this point, I don't plan on having one for myself. I don't even plan on a tombstone or burial. I plan on having my body encased in carbonite like Han Solo and left leaning against a wall somewhere. Obviously, this isn't possible-yet- but one can dream. I'll be donating this marvel of human anatomy, I mean beaten up old body to organ donors and science. Although the eulogies are wonderful to hear, its the stories you hear at the gathering after the funeral that I enjoy. Of course, we mourn-losing a loved one is devastating. But the stories and the laughter and the reverence than ensues afterwards is a reflection, in my opinion, of the impact that this person left on us. What a testament to an individual when we smile, laugh and maybe even want to continue their legacy ourselves.

I believe firmly in celebrating people before they die. But there are times when this isn't possible. As I have learned, our time here can end without notice. I'm not trying to be morbid, rather taking an opportunity to take a moment of pause to consider what I want/need to do before I head to another galaxy.

I can't speak for others, but I can't possibly that I'm unique and that there are so many others like me. I sent a majority of my adulthood in pursuit of happiness. When I say this, I'm talking about the materialistic rewards of life. I busted my ass at work for 50-90 hours a week. I wanted that house and the cool car and the toys. I'm not saying this was the top priority, but it was up there. My biggest goal was to raise two amazing kids, which I am proud to say I have. I'm sure many of us would like to be remembered as a great boss for example. But isn't it more important that we be remembered for being good citizens, charitable, kind and a great parent?

I am surrounded by amazing people who are doing such great things for not only their families, but for their neighbourhoods, their churches, various charities and this great city. On Twitter, there is an account called Kindness

Matters (@KindnessLDNONT) and each day, this account recognizes great people in our community. What has been made clear to me is that not once do they choose someone who is a great boss, rather they focus on people who are doing such amazing things that will leave a huge impact not only today, but for years and years to come. They have featured union leaders, mental health advocates, police officers who work with our youth and so many more. This is what I believe we should be focusing on.

Please do not misunderstand. The efforts in our work world have a huge impact on the daily lives of many. I don't care if you're a trauma doctor or a fast food worker-you make a wonderful difference in the world. If you think you don't, give your head a shake. Although I was assholey at times, I know in my heart that I was a good boss. But this shouldn't be my entire legacy.

In the last couple of years, I've done some selfish and crappy things. I'm not looking for penance, but I've been given an opportunity to make a more positive impact. I plan on being a much better person. I plan on passing along whatever knowledge I have to either help others or at minimum, prevent some from doing what I did. I am taking better care of myself. I've learned to be more patient and respectful thanks to some tough and at times, cruel life lessons. I plan on going back to what I did before-giving back.

I have been forgiven for the wrongs that I committed. Now, I need to practice what I've learned and forgive others. As I said earlier, the past is the past. I can change what I did, and others can't change what they've done. I want to be the funny smartass that people know me to be. I'd like to be the voice of change and stand up for those who need the support. Most importantly, I want to be the dad Sarah and Phillip need me to be. These two young adults will be part of my legacy and I have no doubt they will be far better people than I ever was.

When I'm gone, I don't want people to cry. I'd like people to laugh their asses off at my lifelong silliness. I like to hope they will look at my kids and smile. I hope people say he was a good guy who left a positive footprint on this earth. Isn't this what we all should strive for- to be better people while we're alive?

Now, if you'll excuse me, I need to find someone who knows something about Carbonite.

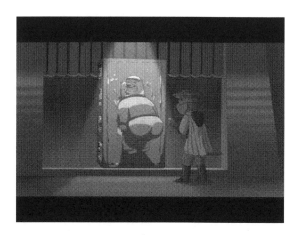

LHSC, Purple Armbands and Violence Policy

I read with some interest this past week about London Health Sciences Centre and concerns about violence (https://www.cbc.ca/news/canada/london/london-health-sciences-centre-purple-armband-policy-labour-minister-1.4908759). And I quote:

"The tool assesses patients at the London Health Sciences Centre for their potential for violence. If they receive a score of moderate or higher, they're forced to wear a purple armband.

For those who refuse, a sign with a large exclamation mark is taped to the doors or curtains of the patient's room to warn staff of the potential risk.
There are further interventions for people in the outpatient mental health section of the hospital. If they refuse to wear the armband, they have to be escorted by staff wherever they go, including the bathroom. And, if they refuse the escort, the patient will be denied treatment that day, according to internal hospital emails obtained by CBC."

Checking out Twitter, I saw some obvious opposition. I too had somewhat of a "WTF" kneejerk reaction. However, after some time to consider this policy, I was starting to see both sides of the argument and both sides have valid points. I'll try and address both sides to the debate. I'm not an expert, however I am certified Levels 1 & 2 in Joint Occupational Health and Safety Committees. I have lengthy experience in H&S and was part of an extensive Workwell Audit.

The Employer: The Occupational Health and Safety Act makes it very clear that employers provide a workplace that is safe from bullying, violence and harassment. Workers have the "Right to Know". Bill 168 furthers addresses workplace violence. The "Internal Responsibility System" requires that **"everyone in the workplace has a role to play in keeping workplaces safe and healthy."**

From the Act: **"Employers, therefore, have specific duties with respect to workplace harassment and workplace violence under the Occupational Health and Safety Act. The harassing or violent person may be someone the worker comes into contact with due to the nature of his or her work. This may include, but is not limited to, a client, customer, volunteer, student, patient, etc. The harassing or violent person may also be part of the workforce, including a co-worker, manager, supervisor or employer. Or the person may be someone with no formal connection to the workplace such as a stranger or a domestic/intimate partner who brings violence or harassment into the workplace. "**

(Source: Https://files.ontario.ca/wpvh_guide_english.pdf)

To take the further, Bill C45 states: **The Westray bill or Bill C-45 was federal legislation that amended the Canadian Criminal Code and became law on March 31, 2004. The Bill (introduced in 2003) established new legal duties for workplace health and safety, and imposed serious penalties for violations that result in injuries or death. The Bill provided new rules for attributing criminal liability to organizations, including corporations, their representatives and**

those who direct the work of others. (Source: https://www.ccohs.ca/oshanswers/legisl/billc45.html)

So, in short, if LHSC fails in their diligence to protect worker's safety, they can be held criminally responsible. I'm sensing that staff have been assaulted, reports filed with WSIB and The Ministry of Labour has warned them as the employer that they need to strengthen their workplace violence policies. I can fully understand and appreciate why this would be done- worker's safety needs to be a top priority. As an employee, don't you want your employer protecting you?

Walk into any emergency, urgent care and even a doctor's office and you'll see signage everywhere that identifies a policy when it comes to aggressive or violent behaviour. During my 30 years in food and beverage, especially the "beverage" portion, I've had to, on numerous occasions, deal with intoxicated patrons. During my years at Western, especially Homecoming games, I've been called upon to play the role of bouncer numerous times. I was a much bigger dude back then and as a rule I can handle myself. But there were too many times when a number of us gorillas had to deal with a violent and drunk customer. Even with training, it sometimes takes 4 or 5 five guys to restrain someone who is impaired. Even with hospital security, I'm sure a number of staff are trained in Crisis Intervention, but one staffer isn't enough to deal with aggressive patients. In short, during my career, I've been assaulted numerous times. Now take this scenario, add in say, mental illness, I would argue that the staff in hospitals are subjected to violence far more than I ever did.

Hospital staff deal with an extraordinary number of patients each day. They do not know, unless they've dealt with a specific patient before, if they have violent tendencies, whether it alcohol or mental health induced. Patients are moved into emergency where a number of staff are present, including doctor's nurses, cleaning staff and porters. A tag indicating a concern is necessary. Staff tag patients who have contagious diseases to protect themselves and visitors warning of the concern, so it makes sense they follow suit with regards to physical concerns.

Now, from a patient's point of view. I don't want to re-hash the details of my various times in the hospitals over the past years, but I will illustrate a few moments where I agree with the hospital in this matter.

Many of us have had to make that dreadful trip to emergency at some point and we've probably witnessed an incident or two when it comes to aggression. A trip to emerg and the longs wait times is enough to drive up stress levels. Sometimes we forget that patients are triaged based on needs-the more traumatic the event, say chest pains, takes precedence over a need for stitches where the wound is temporarily controlled- the bleeding is under control. Sitting in an emergency or urgent care waiting room when you're not feeling good is not an enjoyable experience. One often wonders if they've forgotten about us. Add in staff and service reductions only increases the tension. I'm a dad-what parent hasn't had to make that dreaded trip with a kid suffering from an ear infection who is in agony. Can't image our stress levels weren't low.

In July 2016, after having my leg amputated, I was recovering in my room and discovered that a mentally unstable patient was in the room next to mine. This gentleman had already destroyed his room, removing various equipment and racks off the walls. One afternoon, while laying in my bed, this patient suddenly charged into room. Imagine me laying in this bed, missing a leg-I was feeling vulnerable. He charged at me and a grabbed a crutch and started to yell at him to get out. I ended up swinging my crutch to protect myself. Staff heard this and reacted quite quickly. This man was obviously on the wrong floor, but as staff explained, there was a bed available to him on the mental health ward.

I can state that, during visits to emergency, I have seen a number of violent and aggressive patients. During one visit, a domestic fight broke out and I saw a man assault his partner. Luckily, the emergency had a number of security on staff and being as busy as the emergency is at LHSC, there were a number of police present as well and the situation was controlled quickly, but not before a woman was assaulted. That same night, after being discharged ad waiting for a ride home, I saw EMS and police pull up. The patient, a female, was extremely violent and although restrained, it was obvious she was a hand full.

One more story: during my month long stay on the Mental Health floor at LHSC, I witnessed on more occasions than I can count, a number of extremely aggressive patients. The mental health floor is divided into the 100 ward and the 200 ward. The 200 ward is for the more aggressive patients that require more attentive attention. I was in the 100 ward and one morning, I watched as a young man, waiting for the doors to be unlocked so he could go for a smoke, become extremely agitated as he waited. He started to kick the doors and yell at staff who had no choice but to deal with this behaviour in a manner that the patient did not care for. He was refused the smoke break and escorted to his room. I'm assuming that this only aggravated the situation.

One morning, on my way to the Addictions Group, a female patient was having quite the meltdown. She was yelling and screaming, but not being physically violent. However, her behaviour was concerning to staff and I could see some patients becoming a little scared, one of them running back to their room. This patient was quickly moved to the 200 ward. Staff had a duty to not only protect themselves, but the other patients as well.

I can appreciate why staff would want potentially aggressive and violent patients labeled. Based on their past and present behaviour, some patients have done this to themselves, yes, some beyond their control. But how many of these patients are simply-how do I put this-assholes? Spend time in an emergency-you know what and who I'm talking about.

What concerns me is the quick labeling of someone who is not deserving of such identification. One time, while in emerg, I was in the bathroom and became very disoriented. I started to fall and made quite the racket in the bathroom trying to get up. The door burst open and several staff and security grabbed me, threw me on a stretcher and restrained me. When I explained the situation, I was unrestrained-especially when they saw the prosthetic leg.

One time, while on the Mental Health ward, a patient was objecting to a search of his room while he was not present. He wasn't, in my opinion, being aggressive, yet a label with an exclamation point, meaning aggressive, was soon hanging outside his door. I'm not a professional, but I found this to be unfair. One day, I was having a quiet day in my room writing-really wasn't feeling sociable. A nurse asked what was wrong and I said nothing, just a quiet day. The next day, doctors questioned me as to why I was uncooperative. I wasn't, just relaxing and writing, yet I was labelled.

This is concerning from a patient's point of view. Labelling can be stigmatizing, and I understand that. I would also theorize that there is a potential for behavioural escalation. Unfair labelling can be especially upsetting, and I would hope the guidelines for determining whether or not a purple armband is assigned are fairly rigid. Trying to imagine patients seeing someone with a purple armband would be a little unsettling. Some hospital staff may be too quick to identify someone as a potential concern. However, some patients/visitors have brought this on themselves-this is something that can't be denied.

This is a tough situation to debate. What is more important: staff, patient and visitor safety or an armband on someone who has a history of violence or who is exhibiting violent behaviour? I don't know what the middle ground is. To quote a cheesy line from Star Trek: "The good of the many outweighs the good of the few.... or the one."

Aftermath: Life After Vodka and Suicide

So, here we are……19 months to the day since I had my last drink and killed myself. A quick re-cap on a crazy couple of years:

July 9th, 2016: lost my leg due to infection and alcoholism

November 1, 2016: Suffered a near fatal heart attack

November 6, 2016: to more heart attacks

February 2017: divorce finalized

April 17, 2017: killed myself

May 2017: hospitalized and homeless-have lost almost everything

Oct 2017: part of my other foot amputated.

Can't make this stuff up. Seems so bizarre considering how "normal" my life was for the previous 49 years. Yet, here I am- still alive and better than ever. Seems odd to say, "better than ever", yet it is so very true.

I am surprised that life has turned out the way it has. You'd think that when you hit rock bottom, its all over. Turns out that hitting rock bottom means there is only one way to go-UP. With the support of some great people, I'm now "Gerry 2.0", meaning, in my not so humble opinion, that I'm a much better person than I was ever before. Despite the ailments that occurred in the past, and with a prosthetic leg, I'm actually far happier than I have been in some time.

I learned some lessons along the way:

- Talk to someone who will listen and not judge. Getting my troubles out helped figure out the solutions.

- Don't worry if you get judged or lose people in your circle. Its not worth your time and energy

- You don't need everything in the world to make you happy

- It takes some work to fight your way back, but it is so worth it

- Life is much more pleasurable when you're nice (strange idea huh?)

- Pass along what you've learned-help some avoid what you've gone through

I'm not proud of the things that I've done in the past couple of years, but I'm not ashamed either. I believe that I'm still stomping around this earth on a prosthetic leg for a reason. Apparently, I've still got some work to do and I plan on taking advantage of this time I have left. No, I don't believe there was a moment where the light shone down, and I had an epiphany. I just learned that we are strong, and we can beat back anything.

This is the last chapter in Pantsless Ramblings. I cannot thank you enough for reading along and for your kind support. And yes, there will be a Ramblings 2- apparently, I have lots to say.

Be good to one another. Enjoy life, smile and remember that we are good people.

Now, it's getting cold out- has anyone seen my pants?

Made in the USA
Middletown, DE
30 November 2018